ROBINS SERIES
No 3

MAGIC, DIVINATION AND WITCHCRAFT AMONG THE BAROTSE OF NORTHERN RHODESIA

Robins Series

A Barotse dancer performing the Kayowe dance with the Makishi
character, Nalindele, in the background

Magic, Divination and Witchcraft Among the Barotse of Northern Rhodesia

By

BARRIE REYNOLDS

1963

UNIVERSITY OF CALIFORNIA PRESS

BERKELEY AND LOS ANGELES

PUBLISHED IN THE UNITED STATES OF AMERICA
BY THE UNIVERSITY OF CALIFORNIA PRESS OF
BERKELEY AND LOS ANGELES, CALIFORNIA

PUBLISHED IN GREAT BRITAIN BY
CHATTO AND WINDUS LTD
LONDON

CONTENTS

ILLUSTRATIONS

PLATES

FIGURES

vii

ILLUSTRATIONS

MAPS

TABLES

FOREWORD

IT is curious that of all differences between the races in Central Africa there is none more marked than the difference in attitude towards witchcraft. By Europeans, witchcraft is generally regarded as mere superstition, though there are still occasional reports of witch-doctors being consulted by them. Witchcraft to the European, moreover, is not respectable. To the African however, whether educated or not, witchcraft is of the utmost significance, for even the most highly educated and sophisticated African must constantly be aware of the beliefs and fears of his fellow-Africans. Indeed his own success in life is often attributed to his ability to use witchcraft to his own advantage. Yet it is only a few hundred years ago that witchcraft figured largely in the life of the people in England and that King James I wrote his famous treatise on the subject. Many years will pass before belief in witchcraft among Africans is eradicated, and those who endeavour to understand the African would do well to study this belief. As far as Central Africa is concerned, few studies of witchcraft have previously been published, and the publication of this volume in the Robins Series will, it is believed, help to fill a wide gap in our knowledge and lead to a fuller and deeper understanding of the African.

In writing his preface to the first volume of the Robins Series, my predecessor, Dr. J. Desmond Clark, wrote, 'There is room for a host more of research workers in the fields of the natural sciences and the humanities and for the publication of their results in a form that is readily understandable without sacrificing its scientific accuracy.' The two earlier books in this series were both historical studies and it is fitting that this, the first book of scientific interest to be published in the series, should have been written by a member of the staff of the Rhodes-Livingstone Museum.

Mr. Barrie Reynolds has been Keeper of Ethnography in the Museum for the past seven years. During this time he has made two major field studies : one, a study of the material culture of the Valley Tonga and their neighbours of the Gwembe Valley ; the other, on which he is at present engaged, a wider ethnographic study of the Mashi peoples of South Western Barotseland. As he explains in his Preface, the present study arose fortuitously as a result of a sudden spate of witchcraft cases in Barotseland. There is no doubt that Mr. Reynolds made full use of his opportunity, and the easy and readable style in which he has set down his findings renders his book of considerable interest to laymen, particularly, to those who, in the course of their work, come into contact with witchcraft and wish to obtain a better understanding of this obscure subject and of its effect on the African.

Gervas Clay
Director, Rhodes-Livingstone Museum
Northern Rhodesia

March, 1962

AUTHOR'S PREFACE

THIS report is based on research carried out between January, 1957, and February, 1958, on information and material collected during the witchcraft investigations then being made in Barotseland by the Protectorate Administration. When these investigations began, the writer was already fully committed to a major study of the material culture of the peoples of the Gwembe Valley, a project that owing to the time factor could not be postponed. This research had, therefore, to be treated as a minor project and, as a result, could not be pursued with the thoroughness that the writer would have liked and that it deserved.

The first brief visit in January, 1957, to Kalabo, to which district the investigations were then confined, was made with the prosaic intention of examining the material confiscated by the magistrate, and of obtaining for the Rhodes-Livingstone Museum such specimens as were of scientific or general interest. During this visit, the extent of the investigations and the value of the information and material they were bringing to light were realized, and arrangements for a further visit were made. In February and March, 1957, two weeks were spent at Kalabo, and a few days each at Mongu, Senanga and Sesheke, where investigations were by then also being made. A preliminary report (Reynolds, 1957) was later produced and distributed to members of the Protectorate Administration. In November, after the main spate of witchcraft prosecutions had fallen off, the writer returned to Barotseland and visited each district in turn to re-examine court case records and other reports, and to discuss the investigations with the officers who had undertaken them.

In January, 1958, Mr. P. J. A. Rigby, who was temporarily in the employ of the Rhodes-Livingstone Institute, was seconded to the Museum and was sent to Barotseland to glean from the court case records of each district certain routine data which were felt to be amenable to statistical analysis. These data and the conclusions drawn from their analysis are to be found in Chapter VII.

The object of this study is the description of the witchcraft and allied practices and beliefs of the peoples of Barotseland.

Obviously, a work of this kind must suffer from certain grave limitations. The time factor has already been mentioned. Secondly, fieldwork proper was not practicable because of the general unrest occasioned by the charges and counter-charges continually being made. A most interesting study, but one which was at the time quite out of the question, would have been of the effect of all this disturbance on village life.

The possession of witchcraft charms, the term, witchcraft, being used in its broadest sense, is in itself a criminal offence and one which, by its reliance on material rather than on verbal evidence, is easily proved or disproved. Accusations based purely on verbal evidence, usually a tangled skein of fact and occult beliefs unacceptable in European courts, are, on the other hand, so difficult to prove that the accused are rarely charged. Almost all cases are, therefore, concerned with such persons—sorcerers, herbal doctors, diviners and witchdoctors—who depend on mechanical aids and *materia medica*. Few if any cases concern those who work without such mechanical aids, as do witches, a few diviners and certain doctors. Similarly, the whole emphasis of the investigation lay on the magico portion of the magico-religious field. Further, as will be seen in Chapter I, the first cases that came to light in Kalabo were murders which had been carried out with *kaliloze* guns ; most of the first hundred accused possessed such guns. As a result, the whole investigation started in a state of unbalance in which the magistrates always kept a very watchful eye open for murder and for the more extreme practices of witchcraft and sorcery.

The magistrates of a district are the District Commissioner and his senior officers. Whilst their judicial functions are important they are intended to occupy only a portion, and not a very major one, of their time. When therefore a boma, the administrative headquarters of a district, finds itself swamped with tens, fifties and then literally hundreds of witchcraft cases, where normally it would deal with four or five a year, there is no time for the pursuit of interesting but nevertheless extraneous information. The District Commissioner and his staff must act as police, magistrates and prison officers and, at the same time as tackling the problems raised by the sudden increase in boma population, must try to continue their routine administrative duties. Small wonder that after the first flush of the enquiry, case records were usually reduced to their essentials. The magistrate pursued only those lines which were judicially fruitful and, in his summary, recorded only those facts which had a direct bearing on the case and thereby on his decision.

AUTHOR'S PREFACE

One of the heartening features of working in a colonial territory is the considerable interest that administrative officers take in the ethnography of the people in their care. The first cases, however, found the Protectorate officers dealing with somewhat unfamiliar beliefs and practices, and it must be confessed that there was very little accessible ethnographic literature to which they could turn. The magistrate was virtually charting unknown seas and his helmsman was his interpreter/clerk or local expert. As cases passed through his court, his knowledge swiftly increased and frequently, no doubt, he would have liked to recall an early case and re-examine the accused in the light of knowledge subsequently gained. Time and expediency did not allow and this report has thereby lost a great deal.

The limitations of this study have been enumerated in some detail, perhaps in too much detail, but it is felt that this is necessary in view of the rather unique environment in which the research was undertaken. This report does, however, benefit from the fact that information was gathered on the witchcraft practices of some thirty or more tribes belonging to various tribal groups. It correlates data obtained by six different magistrates in five different parts of the Protectorate.

The writer has, since 1957, had the pleasure of reading Turner's (1957) book on the Ndembu and he feels that to set this report, based as it is on an abnormal eruption, in its proper context, it should be read in conjunction with the social dramas narrated by Turner. Without such a corrective it is feared that the following pages will present a distorted picture of life in the Protectorate.

I am grateful to the Secretary to the Ministry of Legal Affairs and Attorney General for permission to publish data obtained from court records and to the Resident Commissioner, Barotseland, for permission to consult files and records and to publish data extracted from them. I am also grateful to the Director, the Rhodes-Livingstone Institute, for the services of Mr. P. J. A. Rigby as a research assistant, and to the Director and Trustees of the Rhodes-Livingstone Museum for permission to undertake this study.

The manuscript in its early stages was read by Professor M. Gluckman and in its final draft by Miss E. M. Shaw and by Messrs. G. C. R. Clay, J. O. Lemon and C. M. N. White. I am especially grateful for their valuable comments and advice.

The Rev. E. Berger generously allowed me to make use of his notes on Chokwe divining baskets, while Mr. C. M. N. White very kindly allowed me to read the manuscript of his paper 'Elements in Luvale Beliefs and Rituals' (1961).

I am deeply indebted to the Resident Commissioner and his staff, particularly Messrs. R. I. Cunningham, J. G. Lawrance, J. O. Lemon, R. J. N. March and I. H. Wethey, for their unfailing patience, advice and help throughout. Without their assistance this study would not have been possible. I am also indebted to the late Mr. Justice A. G. C. Somerhough, o.b.e., q.c., for his help during the early months of the investigations.

Numerous other people have also assisted either with advice or information throughout my research but it would be impossible to list them all. I must, therefore, content myself with offering them my deepest thanks for their help and co-operation.

In conclusion, I would like especially to thank Mr. P. J. A. Rigby for gathering the statistical data for Chapter VII and Mr. M. Yeta for providing the illustrations. To my wife, who has assisted me throughout, I am also indebted. Her constant help and encouragement have eased considerably the task of preparing this work. For this I am deeply grateful.

ACKNOWLEDGEMENTS

I am grateful to the following publishers and editors, and authors, for permission to quote passages verbatim from books and articles in the bibliography below:

Messrs. Edward Arnold, from C. Gouldsbury and H. Sheane, *The Great Plateau of Northern Rhodesia*.

Central Africa House Press and Messrs. J. T. Munday, E. M. Vowles, and G. W. Broomfield, *Witchcraft*.

Clarendon Press and the Editor, *The Shorter Oxford Dictionary*.

Clarendon Press and Professor E. E. Evans-Pritchard, *Witchcraft, Oracles and Magic among the Azande*.

Commission for Technical Cooperation in Africa South of the Sahara, the Scientific Council for Africa South of the Sahara (CCTA/CSA) and Dr. M. J. Field, *Witchcraft as a primitive interpretation of mental disorder*.

Mr. Geoffrey Cumberlege and the Oxford University Press, the Rhodes-Livingstone Institute and Professors E. Colson and M. Gluckman, *Seven Tribes of British Central Africa*.

The Editor and Mlle. M. Kuntz, *Les rites occultes et la sorcellerie sur le Haut-Zambèze*, in Journal de la Société des Africanistes.

The Editors from the late M. Th. Delachaux, *Méthode et Instruments de divination en Angola*, in Acta Tropica.

Federal Broadcasting Corporation of Rhodesia and Nyasaland, *Listeners' Letters*.

Robert Hale Ltd. and Mr. G. Hogg, *Cannibalism and Human Sacrifice*.

Messrs. E. Hawkins and the Rev. F. S. Arnot, *Garenganze*.

Juta and Co. Ltd. and Dr. M. Gelfand, *Medicine and Magic of the Mashona*.

The Rhodes-Livingstone Institute and Professor M. Gluckman, *Economy of the Central Barotse Plain*.

Lutterworth Press and the Rev. W. Holman Bentley, *Pioneering on the Congo*.

Macmillan and Co. Ltd., and the Rev. E. W. Smith and Mr. A. M. Dale, *The Ila-speaking peoples of Northern Rhodesia*.

Manchester University Press and the Rhodes-Livingstone Institute,
and Professor M. Gluckman, *The Judicial Processes among the Barotse of Northern Rhodesia*;
and Dr. W. V. Turner, *Schism and Continuity in an African Society*; *Ndembu Divination, its Symbolism and Techniques*;
and Mr. C. M. N. White, *Elements in Luvale Beliefs and Rituals*.

Methuen and Co. Ltd. and Dr. K. Birket-Smith, *The Eskimos*.

The Editor and Mr. H. Tracey, *The Bones*, in Nada.

ACKNOWLEDGEMENTS

Northern Rhodesia Government,
    The Forest Department, and Messrs. D. B. Fanshawe and C. D. Hough,
    Poisonous Plants of Northern Rhodesia.
    The Department of Labour, *Annual Report for the Year, 1957.*
    The Ministry of Native Affairs, *Annual Report for the Year, 1957.*
    The Ministry of Native Affairs, the Rhodes-Livingstone Institute, and Mr.
    S. A. Symon, *Some Notes on the Preparation and Use of Native Medicines
    in the Mankoya District.*

Oxford University Press, the International African Institute,
    and Dr. M. McCulloch, *The Southern Lunda and Related Peoples*;
    and Dr. W. V. Turner, *The Lozi Peoples of North-Western Rhodesia*;
    and Dr. G. Wagner, *The Bantu of Northern Kavirondo*;
    and Mr. C. M. N. White, *Witchcraft, Divination and Magic among the
    Balovale Tribes*, in Africa.

Oxford University Press Inc. and Professor H. E. Sigerist, *Primitive and Archaic
Medicine.*

Rhodes University and Professor P. Mayer, *Witches.*

Routledge and Kegan Paul Ltd.,
    and the Editorial Committee of the Royal Anthropological Institute of
    Great Britain and Ireland, *Notes and Queries on Anthropology*;
    and Professor I. Schapera, *The Khoisan Peoples of South Africa.*

Seeley Service and Co. Ltd. from the late Mr. F. M. Melland, *In Witchbound
Africa.*

University of Cape Town,
    and Dr. E. Ashton, *Medicine, Magic and Sorcery among the Southern Sotho*;
    and Miss D. F. Bleek, *Naron, a Bushman Tribe of the Central Kalahari.*

C. A. Watts and Co. Ltd. from the late Sir J. G. Frazer, *Magic and Religion.*

Witwatersrand University Press, the Editorial Board,
    and the Rev. W. Singleton-Fisher, *Black Magic Feuds*, in African Studies.

I am also grateful to the Federal Ministry of Health, Salisbury, for per-
mission to reproduce the X-ray photograph on Plate IV, and to the Northern
Rhodesia Information Department for permission to reproduce the frontispiece,
Plate II and the flooded homestead on Plate III.

NOTE ON VERNACULAR TERMS

WITH one exception (*muloi*, pl. *baloi*) vernacular words are used in the singular, irrespective of their context. The names of tribes are given in root form, prefixes being omitted. The name, Barotse, which is the sole exception, is employed both as the adjective derived from Barotseland, and as the noun meaning the inhabitants of Barotseland. It is not used as a synonym for Lozi.

Most of the vernacular terms used throughout this book are in common usage over a wide area and among many different tribes. Except in a few special cases, no attempt is made to trace the origin of each term or to ascribe it to a particular language. Where a term is stated in the text to be Lozi or Luyana, it must be remembered that the present Lozi language is of Kololo origin, though a number of Luyi words are still employed.

CHAPTER I

INTRODUCTION

The Protectorate

As may be seen from the accompanying map, Barotseland Protectorate, which covers an area of 48,798 square miles, lies between the parallels 22° and 26° East and 14° and 18° South and is roughly rectangular in shape, though with the south-western corner excised. The heart of Loziland, however, is the central Barotse flood plain (*bulozi*) which extends along the Zambezi approximately between 14½° and 16° South and is some 120 miles in length. At its widest part it is some 25 miles across. Minor arms of this plain reach out into the surrounding forest along the tributaries of the main river.

The ruler of the Protectorate is the Litunga or Paramount Chief, Sir Mwanawina III, whose father, Lewanika, was responsible in 1890 and in 1900 for obtaining for his people the protection of the British Crown by means of treaties.[1] These treaties reserved for the Barotse people certain rights and privileges which they today still enjoy. The Administration of the Protectorate is, however, in many ways similar to that of the Provinces of Northern Rhodesia. The Resident Commissioner at Mongu represents the Northern Rhodesia Government and advises the Paramount Chief on more crucial matters, and the Protectorate is divided up into five districts, each of which is controlled by a District Commissioner aided by up to three junior European officers. Three of these district headquarters (bomas), Mongu, Kalabo and Senanga, are situated on the very edge of the flood plain. The fourth, Sesheke, is placed close to the pontoon which links Katima Mulilo and the Caprivi Strip, which is administered by South-West Africa, to the north or, at that point, east bank of the Zambezi. The fifth boma, Mankoya, is situated 150 miles east of Mongu and controls a district which, perhaps by reason of its exclusion from the Zambezi and from the flood plain, is withdrawn a little from the rest of Barotseland. Formerly, there was a sixth district in the Protectorate, Balovale, but in 1941 this was excised and attached to North-Western Province.

---

[1] The Lochner Concession, 1890, and the Lewanika Concession, 1900.

By comparison with progress in the rest of Northern Rhodesia, europeanization of the Protectorate is slow and the contrast of Bantu practising primitive agriculture and the new world of aeroplanes, motor pontoons and radio telephones, is sometimes rather startling. The term europeanization is used here in its cultural sense. There is no European settlement other than Government posts, mission stations and trading stores of which the two latter are established on land loaned by, or leased from the Paramount Chief.

It would, however, be wrong to underestimate the importance of the part played by foreign influences, both European and African, in changing and reshaping the traditional culture. This effect is to be seen not only in the more material aspects of the culture but also in the non-material, including those of magic and witchcraft. The beliefs and fears of other tribes have been absorbed and, at the same time, the devices and techniques of their sorcerers, their doctors and their diviners adopted. The effect of contact with urban and industrial environments frequently takes the form of conflict between the old and the new and the resultant tension all too often finds expression in accusations of witchcraft. Let us, therefore, begin by examining the extent and importance of this contact with the outside world. It will also be necessary to examine the inhabitants of the Protectorate themselves in order to appreciate the wide variety of tribes they represent and of cultures to which they belong.

Communications and Migrant Labour

The Zambezi may justifiably be called the artery of Barotseland. Throughout most of the year it is possible to move by barge, launch or canoe along the whole length of the river channels through the plain and even up some of the tributaries. When the floods are up, the plain is almost completely covered by water and, for all but the largest craft, channels lose their importance and the shortest and most direct routes may be chosen. A few miles below Senanga, rapids and minor falls block the route and compel travellers to use the road which follows the west bank to Katima Mulilo. Here the river is again navigable and boats ply down to Mambova, 48 miles from Livingstone.

It is by the river, the Labour Route[1] and the Mankoya/Machili

[1] The Labour Route runs from Mongu to Machili (see map) and is used by those travellers unable or unwilling to use public transport. Camps are set at intervals of roughly a day's march along its length to give shelter to these travellers.

road that rural Africans, mainly young men attracted by prospects of urban life and wages, find their way to Livingstone, the nearest town. Lusaka, which lies 450 miles east of Mongu, is rather too far for the impecunious labourer or young lad seeking his fortune. In

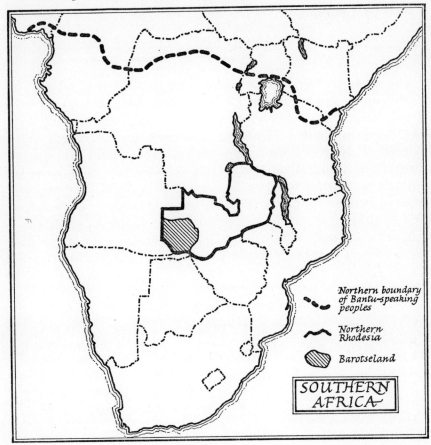

Northern boundary
of Bantu-speaking
peoples

Northern
Rhodesia

Barotseland

SOUTHERN
AFRICA

any case, during the rains this line of communication is always disrupted.

Table 1[1] shows the extent of the annual flow to and from the towns. The figures relate to both sexes and include children.

There is a certain amount of movement backwards and forwards across the Angolan border; this consists either of migrants attracted by tales of greater opportunities in the British territory, or of travellers making short trips to fulfil social or other obligations.

[1] For these figures I am indebted to the Labour Officer, Livingstone.

3

TABLE 1

Movement into and out of Barotseland; July 1956–June 1957

	TO	FROM	TOTAL
a. Livingstone	12,156	15,192	27,348
b. Lusaka	465	326	791
Total	12,621	15,518	28,139

The strongest rivals to Livingstone for the supply of labour are the recruiting organizations. Of these there were, in 1957, two—Ulere,[1] recruiting labour on a non-return basis for farming and other work in Southern Rhodesia, and more important, the Witwatersrand Native Labour Association (colloquially known as Wenela), recruiting labour[2] on a return basis for periods of twelve to eighteen months for work on the mines of the Rand. Not only are these labourers brought back to Barotseland at the completion of their contract, but payment of part of their wages is compulsorily deferred until their homecoming and is then paid out at the disembarkation point. Many workers, during their absence from home,

TABLE 2

Deferred pay and remittances of migrant Wenela workers, 1957

	DEFERRED PAY	REMITTANCES
Balovale	—	£242 0s 0d
Kalabo	£22,566 11s 10d	7,559 0s 0d
Katima Mulilo	5,254 8s 5d	3,440 0s 0d
Mongu	17,712 9s 0d	3,016 0s 0d
Senanga	11,146 10s 0d	2,555 0s 0d
District Commissioners (at places where there is no W.N.L.A. office)	—	463 0s 0d
	£56,679 19s 3d	£17,275 0s 0d

(Northern Rhodesia Government, 1958b)

[1] Ulere has since ceased activities. During the period, July 1956 to June 1957, 3,985 labourers were recruited and transported to Southern Rhodesia. 1,154 made use of Ulere transport to return to Barotseland. Personal communication; Labour Officer, Livingstone.

[2] During the calendar year 1957, 3,600 men were recruited from Barotseland and Balovale, and 3,553 were returned on completion of their contracts. (Northern Rhodesia Government, 1958b).

voluntarily allot money to their dependants and this is paid out regularly at the local Wenela office. The earnings of the migrant Wenela workers play an important part in the general economy of Barotseland, as may be seen from Table 2.

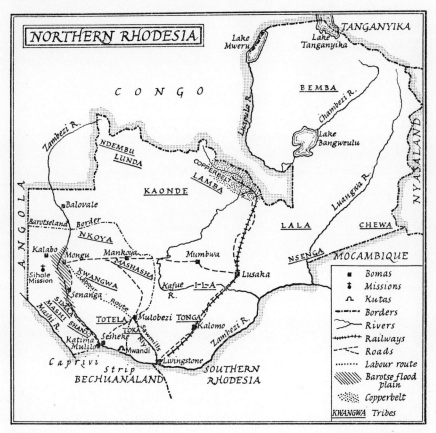

Although not all of this money was paid out to Barotse residents, for example at Balovale, Katima Mulilo and by the District Commissioners, it will be appreciated that this must still represent a considerable part of the total cash income of the inhabitants of the Protectorate. When considering these figures one must also bear in mind that the minimum unskilled labour rate payable in the Protectorate at that time was 2s per day. Prior to February, 1957, it was only 1s 8d per day.

The pecuniary incentive is, therefore, considerable for the fit young man seeking adventure, the excitements of an urban life and a rapid rise in his social status. Wenela not only affords all these but also starts its recruits off in their new life with the thrill of travelling by aeroplane for the first leg of their journey to Francistown, Bechuanaland, where they entrain for the Rand.

Population and Tribal Groupings

The population of the Protectorate was estimated in 1957 to be as follows:

TABLE 3

Population statistics, 1957 (i)

Mongu	92,053
Kalabo	71,695
Mankoya	41,077
Senanga	59,155
Sesheke	32,166
Total	296,146

and to be composed of the following:

TABLE 4

Population statistics, 1957 (ii)

1. *Adults:*

Male-Taxable		67,778
	Exempt	17,397
	Total	85,175
	Female	104,576

2. *Children:*

Male	56,590
Female	49,805

3. *Totals:* 296,146

(Northern Rhodesia Government, 1958a)

Of the 67,778 taxable males, 20,136 were at work outside Barotseland, no doubt accompanied by a substantial number of women and children.

Gluckman, in his survey of the tribes of the Protectorate (1941),

6

lists some twenty-five tribes which together form the bulk of the population. There are a number of minor groups which Gluckman notes but excludes from his classification. To include these and other minor groups the following amended classification is proposed.

TABLE 5

The tribes of Barotseland

LUYANA (108,537)

Lozi (50,811); Kwandi (14,080); Kwangwa (37,696); Mwenyi (4,370); Mbowe (1,580).

ASSIMILATED LUYANA (43,199)

Nyengo (7,990), including Lutwi and Lyuwa (1,574); Makoma (9,506); Imilangu (7,199), including Ndundulu; Mishulundu (?); Simaa (7,737); Yei or Makoba (140); Shanjo (3,219); Old Mbunda (?, see under LUNDA-LUVALE below); Mashi (4,661); Mpukushu (394); Fwe (1,387); Kangala (635); Kwangali (331); Mulonga (?).

LUNDA-LUVALE (47,506)

Luvale (23,249); Chokwe (5,023); Luchazi (12,694); New Mbunda (?); Yauma (2,846); Mbalango or Mbalangwe (769); Lunda/Ndembu (1,361); Mbwela (?); Kaonde (1,564).

(N.B. Mbunda, including both Old and New, are given in the 1957 figures as 32,985).

NKOYA (23,788)

Nkoya (17,484); Mashasha (5,844); Lukolwe (?); Lushange (460).

BANTU-BOTATWE (33,595)

Ila (247); Tonga (?); Toka (11,087); Totela (14,181); Subya (8,080).

OTHERS (6,536)

Non-Bantu—Bushmen (?)
Foreign—Ndebele (Matabele), Tswana, Humbe, Zulu, Ngoni, Nyanswa, Swahili, etc., in small numbers.

This classification is followed in this report. Where the terms, LUYANA, ASSIMILATED LUYANA, LUNDA-LUVALE, NKOYA, BANTU-BOTATWE, are used in small capitals, they refer to the groups of tribes listed above.

As will be realized from the foregoing, the cultural picture in Barotseland is the most complicated in Northern Rhodesia and among the most complicated in central Africa. As Gluckman (1941) points out, 'Within Barotseland each tribal group tended to have one or more areas where it was the nuclear community of the district but members of most tribes lived in nearly every part of the country, and especially in Loziland itself.' The southward movement of the LUNDA-LUVALE peoples during the last few centuries affected Barotseland just as it did other parts of south-central Africa. The counter-movements, in the nineteenth century, of the Kololo and Ndebele also had considerable effects on culture and tribal distribution. The returning Luyi (Lozi), whilst they wiped out the over-lords almost completely, could not restore the old order or prevent the intermingling of the vassal tribes; in fact, they preferred them to mingle so that they might the more easily be welded into a homogeneous nation. The demands of domestic policy whereby groups were moved from one area to another, for example Nkoya and Toka to Kalabo, complicated the picture. Foreign policy too, by the assimilation of captured slaves taken in raids on neighbouring tribes, added further complications. In this century, the steady eastward and south-eastward immigration and infiltration of tribes from Angola, such as the Luvale and Mbunda, are producing further important changes. In fact, the metaphor of a cultural picture is inappropriate and the whole is more accurately likened to a tangled skein of wool.

The Lozi domestic aim, of a nation composed of the heterogeneous collection of Lozi and vassal tribes welded into one, is dealt with thoroughly by Gluckman (1951) and there is no need here for further elaboration. He has elsewhere discussed (1941) what is perhaps one of the most interesting products of this policy, the division of labour or rather skills on a tribal and area basis. This division has created a web of economic interdependence between the tribes and especially between the dwellers of the plain and those of the surrounding bush. Speaking very generally it may be said that the plain dwellers keep cattle, specialize in fishing, and have maize as their staple cereal. They necessarily practise transhumance of their cattle and themselves migrate annually from the flood plain to the surrounding forest fringe. The bush people keep few or no cattle, are much more dependent on their crops of cassava and bullrush millet, and lay more stress on the importance of hunting and food gathering. Similarly, crafts are determined by the sources of the raw materials; woodworking, smelting, smithing and the like being bush crafts, and mat-making, boat-building and fishing being plain crafts.

Generalizing further, it may be said that except in important centres, such as Limulunga, Lealui and the boma townships, the tribal population may be divided between plain and bush. The LUYANA, with the outstanding exception of the Kwangwa, are plain dwellers; the NKOYA and LUNDA-LUVALE are bush dwellers. The ASSIMILATED LUYANA and the rest are scattered throughout both, though the Bushmen, the Shanjo, the Mashi and so on are only to be found in the south-west. The LUYANA, most of the ASSIMILATED LUYANA, the NKOYA and, of the BANTU-BOTATWE, the Totela and Subya have the main bodies of their tribes within the kingdom. All the others are minor offshoots of main bodies resident outside. All the inhabitants of the Protectorate, whatever their tribe, owe allegiance to the Paramount Chief and are thereby entitled to call themselves Lozi. Residence is predominantly virilocal though not necessarily patrilocal.

The Paramount Chief, like many of his people, resides during the dry season in the plain itself—at his capital Lealui. When the floods rise he moves out to his second capital, Limulunga, which stands on the edge of the plain. To the south, at Nalolo in Senanga district, is the next most important capital where the Mulena Mukwae, a royal princess, lives. Libonda, the capital of Kalabo district, is the seat of the much less important princess, Mulena Mbowanjikana. There are also capitals at Naliele and Mwandi to control Mankoya and Sesheke districts respectively and, until 1947, there was also a capital at Kaunga which was intended to guard the south-west and to control the Mashi area. Each district is split up into sub-districts, each administered by a *kuta* or council of *indunas*.

The population falls into a number of classes: Royalty (descendants from all Paramounts through males or females for some four or five generations) together with their affines; freemen (theoretically including all tribes); and, prior to the European administration, slaves and serfs. Certain tribes in the outlying areas, for example, the Mashasha in Mankoya, have their own chief who leads the *kuta*, but in the heart of Barotseland there is but one real chief, the Paramount. Assimilated immigrant groups have to be content with a senior *induna* as their leader.

In common with most central African peoples, the Barotse (used in the widest sense) hold a belief in a High or Supreme God, usually

9

termed Lesa or Nyambe. Whilst he is the ultimate source of power he is generally considered to be remote from petty human affairs. Ancestral spirits, on the other hand, are closely concerned with the affairs and behaviour of their descendants and are accorded due respect in the form of offerings of beer and food at appropriate times. Among the LUNDA-LUVALE these spirits have a particularly important role in association with the *mukanda* initiation schools. Graduates of the schools dress in elaborate painted masks and costumes, intended to represent the spirits, and dance and carry out the duties assigned by tradition to each of the characters. Both spirits and dancers are termed *makishi*.

Each deceased is considered to leave behind a spirit (*mukishi*, LUNDA-LUVALE; *silumba*, LUYANA). Information on the nature of this spirit and its subsequent behaviour is inadequate, but it would seem that while normally this spirit becomes an ancestral spirit, it can also be seized by a magician and used as a familiar. Whether this is an alternative fate, whether such a spirit has more than one facet, or whether each person possesses more than one spirit is not at all clear.

Ancestral spirits, while they also protect the interests of their descendants, can on occasion punish them should they be displeased or wish to draw attention to themselves. Such punishment usually takes the form of possession of the descendant and consequent illness ; it may be employed if the ancestor feels neglected, wishes to have his name perpetuated by a newly born child or wishes his descendant to succeed him in a particular craft or pursuit. There are in addition other spirits, for example that of *muba*, which inhabit the bush and lie in wait for the unwary. Again, however, data is very scanty.

These are but brief notes.[1] To obtain a more complete understanding of the cultural background of this kingdom, one must look to the works of Colson, Gluckman, Melland, Turner and White. Against these must be set the following exposition of witchcraft, sorcery and divining practices. The external pressures and internal attractions which have caused and still cause immigration of foreign groups from different directions and culture areas ; the interaction between these groups and the autochthonous people and between one another in their restless movements within the kingdom ; the even more foreign influences brought in by migrant labourers re-

[1] Drawn primarily from Gluckman (1941 and 1951), McCulloch (1951) and Turner (1952).

turning from the far world of urban and industrial southern Africa : all these have stirred up supernatural beliefs and have multiplied the mythical creatures that prey on the fears and suspicions of the local people.

Basically, the causes of these fears and tensions have remained unaltered. It is only the methods and beliefs that have been affected. One can still trace accusations to root causes, such as envy of good crops, of possessions or good fortune, social and political ambition, eccentricity and malice, harsh words in quarrels and just plain ill luck or bad management. To these must be added the restlessness provoked by tastes of urban freedom and also the current unbalance of monetary and social values resulting from migrant labour. The tension that results from the conflicting claims on his income of the young worker himself and of his seniors and dependants in his home village, does little to ease the problem. It is perhaps significant that the spark that touched off this investigation was exploded literally by returning migrant labourers.[1]

History of the Investigations

On the 2nd of October, 1956, the District Commissioner, Kalabo, was informed by one of the Roman Catholic missionaries at Sihole Mission, of rumours in circulation that two women had recently been murdered and that the crimes were in some way connected with witchcraft. Investigation proved this rumour to be correct and the District Commissioner was fortunate enough to lay hands not only on the murderers but also on the two corpses. The victims had been shot at fairly close range with short-barrelled homemade muzzle-loaders, commonly known as *kaliloze* night guns.

Confessions by the murderers and information subsequently obtained led to the arrest of other gunmen. These were frequently found to be flourishing witchdoctors having in their possession not only *kaliloze* guns but also human skulls, limb bones and, in a few cases, reputedly human flesh. Other killings were, therefore, suspected.

The investigation progressed rapidly in snowball fashion. Confessions and volunteered information soon led to the arrest of more men possessing incriminating material. This in turn led to still more arrests. During the last quarter of the year, the two subordinate

[1] It would appear that several of these had lucrative practices as witchdoctors, diviners and herbal doctors whilst in Johannesburg.

courts in Kalabo district heard 94 cases involving 102 persons resulting from these investigations, and 5 men were on remand
awaiting trial in the High Court in connection with the two original
murders. It is to be noted that the total number of cases of all kinds
heard in 1956 in the two subordinate courts was only 145.

The resources of the District Commissioner proving inadequate
to deal with the inundation, African police, prison warders and extra
messengers were brought into the district. The aid of the Criminal
Investigation Department was also requested and an European
officer assigned to the investigation.

When informing the District Commissioner of the deaths, the
Roman Catholic missionary reported a further vague rumour of
insertions being made under the skin of the chest. This remark bore
fruit a few weeks later when the District Commissioner discovered
short lengths of needle inserted beneath the skin of the chests of
many of the arrested *kaliloze* gunmen. Suspecting a connection between the guns and the needles, he subsequently searched not only
the dwellings of suspects for guns and/or human remains, but also
their persons for evidence of insertions of needles. Similarly, noting
the frequent association of witchcraft or sorcery with *kaliloze* guns,
he included among his suspects any person pretending to deal in
magical matters or possessing 'witchcraft' material.

Besides the considerable number of cases dealt with by the subordinate courts of the District Commissioner and his staff, five cases,
involving eight accused, were serious enough to justify the Resident
Magistrate sitting at Kalabo on the 14th and 15th of January, 1957.
Three of these cases were concerned with attempts to murder, one
with conspiracy to murder, and one with an attempt to procure the
commission of murder.

From the 14th to the 31st of January inclusive, the High Court
sat at Mongu[1] to try three cases of murder. All three murders had
been committed with *kaliloze* guns. Two cases had been sent up
from Kalabo, the third was from Senanga. Even in this last case the
murderer was a Kalabo man. All seven accused were convicted and
sentenced to death. On appeal to the Federal Supreme Court the
sentences were confirmed.

With the entry of the new year there were three developments. In
1956, the investigation had been confined, mainly because of the evidence available, to Kalabo district. In 1957, it spread into all other

[1] For a record of the proceedings see Northern Rhodesia Government, 1957a, b and c.

districts of the Protectorate and even to the contiguous districts of Kalomo and Livingstone. Very soon the emphasis swung away from Kalabo and centred on Senanga and, more important, on Mongu.

Secondly, whereas formerly accusations had usually been oral, letters, mainly anonymous, now began to pour into the bomas. A number merely contained wild accusations and the amount of supporting evidence offered varied considerably. It is surprising, however, how often the writer indicated exactly where incriminating evidence was hidden—in a hole in the ground, in a garden house, and so on. Indeed, if it were not for the suspect's ready acknowledgement of ownership of such material, one might believe it to have been planted by his accusers. At first, each and every accusation, whether oral or written, anonymous or otherwise was, if humanly possible, investigated. After a few months, however, it was considered desirable to restrict attention, in the case of written accusations, only to those made by persons who had signed their names, and to discard anonymous charges.

Thirdly, in Kalabo, in the course of investigating witchcraft allegations, police and administrative officers brought to light cases of alleged necrophagy. This practice, which is again reputed to be associated with murder by witchcraft or sorcery, was later reported from all other districts.

In Mankoya, which the main spate of investigations had left almost untouched, there was a surprising recrudescence late in 1958 when the rest of the Protectorate was returning to normal. Some fifty to sixty cases of necrophagy, brought by irate villagers against their neighbours, suddenly flooded the subordinate courts. The strength of the feelings aroused could be gauged by the amount of manhandling that had occurred before each miscreant arrived at the boma. After this late burst, however, all appears to have settled down to normal, and to date there has been no further outbreak.

CHAPTER II

THE *MULOI*

I N this chapter the meaning of the term *muloi*, and the motives ascribed to him are considered, together with the reasons why accusations of witchcraft are made and why they are so often accepted. Beliefs in necrophagy and its relation to witchcraft are also examined, and the selection and training of witches and sorcerers discussed before, finally, the methods employed by the sorcerer and by the necrophager are described in detail.

The term *muloi*[1] (pl. *baloi*), is commonly translated by both African and European as 'witch'. This is misleading, for the vernacular term includes both 'witch' and 'sorcerer'. Both are believed capable of harming others by magical means but, whereas the former has an inherent power for evil, perhaps unknown even to himself, the latter uses acquired powers, spells, rites or medicines and is very conscious of his activities. As Evans-Pritchard (1950.21) explains for the Azande of East Africa:

> Azande believe that some people are witches and can injure them in virtue of an inherent quality. A witch performs no rite, utters no spell and possesses no medicines. An act of witchcraft is a psychic act. They believe also that sorcerers may do them ill by performing magic rites with bad medicines.

Throughout the investigations, the terms *muloi* and 'witch' were used as synonyms; in this report, however, the above distinction between sorcerers and witches is drawn; the criteria being the presence or known absence of 'rite . . . spell . . . medicine'. As was to be expected, most of the witches prosecuted or mentioned in the court records were in fact sorcerers. When arrests are based on material rather than on verbal evidence such must be the case. The exposure of a supposed witch, as distinct from a sorcerer, is fraught with hazard, for the proof is of a type usually frowned upon by the courts and, in any case, an accusation of witchcraft very often rebounds as a

---

[1] The Lunda, Luvale and Luchazi use *muloji*, while the Chokwe, surprisingly, use *nganga*, a term that is more commonly applied to the witchdoctor or leech. In view of its wide distribution among and general acceptance by most central African tribes, *muloi* is employed throughout this work.

slander or libel case.[1] Although very few cases of witchcraft have come to light during the investigations, it cannot be assumed that Barotse people believe only in sorcery, nor even that this is more commonly practised than is witchcraft. White (1948b.83) considers that the L U N D A-L U V A L E believe in the existence of both witches and sorcerers, 'Among the Lunda, Lwena (Luvale), and Luchazi it is clear that witches work evil in two quite distinct ways—sorcery and inherent evil or inherent witchcraft,' and discusses at some length the methods employed by each. Turner (1952.54) on the other hand, in his survey of the Lozi peoples writes :

I have been unable to find any reference in the literature to witchcraft if witchcraft is defined, as is now customary, as the inherent power of evil. The *baloi* appear to be completely conscious in their malevolence and to work by the use of observable substances as well as by the manipulation of supernatural beings.

It is reasonable to suppose that witches do have a place in Barotse supernatural beliefs. The data is, however, so nebulous and unsatisfactory that the subject must be left open to await further research.

It is of interest to consider the motives behind the attacks of both sorcerers and witches and what they hope to gain by them. Ashton (1943.8) discussing Basuto witches states, 'while they do have a penchant for human flesh and possess familiars they are on the whole harmless creatures that use their powers and medicines for amusement, perverted though this may be.' Mayer (1954.5) in a general essay on the subject considers, 'that witches work from envy, malice or spite, against individuals, rather than in pursuit of material gain as such.' Gelfand (1956.52) too holds this opinion, though it is not clear whether he is referring to witch or sorcerer when discussing the Shona *muroi*.

The *muroi* or witch is a person possessed with an evil spirit wishing to harm others. The essential characteristic of a *muroi* or witch (plural *varoyi*) is not the intention to make someone ill but to kill him. Sometimes she determines to kill a person because she dislikes him or has been offended by him, but more usually she kills because she likes to do so.

While the Azande (Evans-Pritchard, 1950.121) consider :

[1] Unless, of course, the complaint is made to a district officer or police officer. For an example of such slander cases *vide* Turner (1957.157. Social Drama V).

a man cannot help being a witch; it is not his fault that he is born with witch-craft in his belly. He may be quite ignorant that he is a witch and quite innocent of acts of witchcraft. In this state of innocence he might do someone an injury unwittingly, but when he has on several occasions been exposed by the poison oracle he is then conscious of his powers and begins to use them, with malice.

Field (1958.2) has found similar beliefs in Ghana; 'she has no con-ceivable motive. She kills and injures, not those to whom it would be natural to wish harm or death, but those in whose well-being she may even have an interest.' Amusement, malice, aimless viciousness, each are ascribed as motives and White (1948b.84) suggests a fourth:

Vandumba (LUNDA-LUVALE familiars) live on the lives of people and this is the price they demand for the services which they render to their owner in bringing him goods or other things which he wants. The owner cannot refuse to let her *ndumba* kill, otherwise it will turn and kill her. Thus the familiar spirit is complete master of its owner, and once he has acquired *ndumba* a person can do little to help himself. The *ndumba* plays havoc with the community whilst the owner reaps his reward but always with the fear of detection.

So far as Barotse witches are concerned I would consider that they are motivated by malice or by familiars beyond their control, as both White and Melland (1923.204–207) suggest.

The data on LUYANA and ASSIMILATED LUYANA beliefs is in-adequate, though the few appropriate case records that give any in-dication at all, mention malice or envy as the motive. Attacks made by sorcerers are mostly intended to cause the illness and death of the victim. There are a few malicious exceptions; for example, the killing of cattle, the aborting of pregnant women, the bringing of unseasonable rain or drought, the crippling of a man's sexual prowess, the reduction of his wealth or prestige. These do not, however, materially affect the main picture; the sorcerer's primary object is the death of his victim and the most common motive for this, and in-deed for his practising sorcery at all, is personal aggrandizement in the face of, and at the expense of his enemies and rivals. By putting his skill, for a consideration, at the disposal of aggrieved clients, a successful sorcerer obtains not only fame, perhaps notoriety is a more appropriate word, but also wealth. When he so wishes, he can use his craft on his own account to remove somebody who prevents his inheritance of further wealth, who blocks his political or social climb, or who possesses some object which he desires for himself.

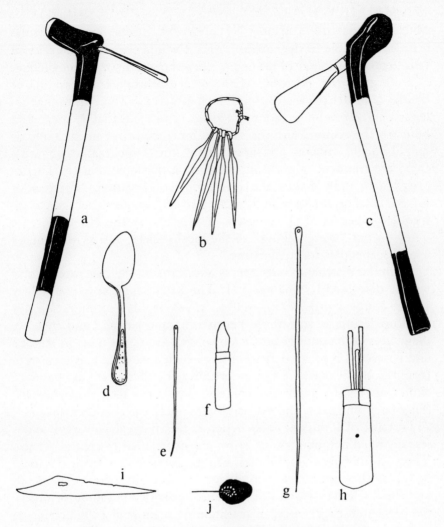

Fig. 1. The tools and implements of the necrophager

a. Dancing hoe
b. Bemba finger knives
c. Axe
d. European dessert spoon

e. Small matting needle (spork)
f. Small LUNDA-LUVALE knife
g. Large matting needle (spork)
h. Points (sporks) in sheath
i. LUNDA-LUVALE knife blade

j. Sewing needle set in a ball of beeswax; small red seed beads are impressed in the wax.

Specimens a–i are used at feasts; j is used to kill the victim. Specimen b is not of Barotse origin but is included for comparative purposes.

Petty revenge after a dispute, or in envy of another's good fortune are also available to the sorcerer, and it would seem that he seldom fails to take advantage of his neighbours or of his superior knowledge.

So argues the African.[1] The social anthropologist would, of course, consider the ascription of such motives and actions to the sorcerer a *post hoc* rationalization of tensions and feuds that had occurred between the accused and the victim. Since both live in the same or neighbouring villages and are usually kin (Gluckman, 1951.76), there are frequent opportunities for such tensions to arise. Turner (1957.150–151) makes the interesting observation, 'Persons of mixed tribal origin, or who have been reared among other tribes, are frequently regarded as sorcerers or witches by the Ndembu. . . . They do not "quite belong" to the local society, and as such make useful scapegoats for misfortune.'

A similar distrust of outsiders is noticeable in the case records and will be discussed in Chapter VII. The Lozi belief, as expressed by Kuntz (1932.136)[2] among others, 'C'est depuis l'immigration des ma-Lubalé que la sorcellerie fleurit plus que jamais,' and that the magicians of the immigrant LUNDA-LUVALE are the most numerous and powerful, must in part stem from such a view. It may also stem from the belief that one's more primitive neighbours must be more skilled in magic, especially sorcery. The Lozi look down on the Angolan immigrants and yet fear their supernatural knowledge.

Distrust of foreigners and belief in the magical powers of one's less civilized neighbours are by no means peculiar to central Africa. The painfully slow assimilation of foreigners, either from the town or from other countries, into village life in many parts of England and the difficulty, which solitary Europeans living among primitive peoples often experience, in maintaining a rational disbelief in the magical powers of their neighbours are closely comparable.

Lane Poole (ms.) with reference to the Nsenga and their neighbours of the Eastern Province of Northern Rhodesia, suggests a

---

[1] See, for example, Gluckman (1955.98).

[2] Kuntz also notes that Paramount Chief Lewanika exiled to the Matabele Plain all those suspected of witchcraft or sorcery. Gluckman (1955.97) was informed, 'Partly under the missionaries' influence King Lewanika declared that charges of sorcery were lies fostered by hate and envy. He sent accused sorcerers to colonize the Matabele Plain between the Zambezi and Mashi Rivers and pointed to their prosperity there as proof of their innocence. . . . He banned the poison ordeal in 1891, and trials for sorcery and witchcraft in 1892.' Jalla (1961.62) records that the use of the poison ordeal and the practice of burning sorcerers was banned in 1889.

number of possible motives behind accusations of witchcraft or sorcery :

Fear: either because of the threats of the accused or because he has performed some unnatural act (such as incest) which places the lives of his kin in jeopardy.

Revenge: Lane Poole quotes the following cases :

A charged B with causing the death of his children by witchcraft. A few years later B brought a similar accusation against A. The motive was retaliation.

In a Kunda case defendant's mother was sick, and in a Nsenga case defendant's mother died. In both cases accusations of witchcraft were preferred and upon investigation the motive was shewn to be retaliation for previous quarrels.

Whether the accuser himself appreciates that his motive is revenge is not stated ; probably he does not, being conscious only of 'bad blood' between the accused and himself.

Disparity of circumstances; for example:

Defendant had a good crop of maize, Complainant a bad one; hence a charge of witchcraft against the former.

A polygamist found himself potent in his relations with one of his wives, impotent in his intercourse with the other. An allegation of witchcraft was made against the former wife of being the cause of his disability.

Disparity of circumstances is a very common reason behind accusations of witchcraft and is recorded by many writers. Thus, Turner (1957.151) discussing an Ndembu accusation :

She, like Sandombu, had been a prodigiously hard worker in her gardens, knew where to plant her crops so that she would obtain a higher yield than other people, and often went on working in the heat of the day when others had retired to gossip in the kitchens. And so the inevitable question was posed: from what sources did she draw her energy and why were her crops better than anyone else's? Obviously she had supernatural powers which gave her outstanding strength and luck.

Where a disease or death is mysterious and inexplicable and where a series of such illnesses or deaths occur: This is one of the most important motives in Lane Poole's list for it is the immediate reason for the accusation. A suspected *muloi* may live at peace with his or her neighbours for a long period and nothing be done. Once the *muloi* is divined as being the cause of a particular trouble, however, the onus is on the victim or his kin to take action; they may not do this for months or perhaps even years.

My brother ACC. 3 LIFU had spoken to me before my mother's death of this trouble, that my mother was bewitching his children, but long before my mother's death—2 or 3 years ago. He said to me then he had been to a witch-diviner, and had been advised that my mother was the one who had finished his ACC. 3's children by bewitching them. (Northern Rhodesia Government, 1957a.4.)

The accused in this case had already lost three children, all, he believed, because of his mother's witchcraft; yet he waited for two to three years, living the while in the same village as his mother and losing during that time another two children, before he took action and employed a *kaliloze* gunman/doctor to kill her. The mental stress Lifu must have undergone during these years must have been considerable. The loss of his children, the realization of his mother's apparent wickedness and the gradual crystallization of his determin-ation to stop her evil attacks must have proved a strain very hard to bear; yet there is no indication that he proclaimed his mother's vil-lainy in public nor went about making wild accusations, nor did he move to another village.

Where the accused is believed to be in possession of severable parts of the victim such as hair and nail clippings. These are considered to be especially potent: To this may be added:

(*a*) any human bones or other remains (such as reputedly human fat or a placenta). The possession of these shows that the owner is dabbling seriously in black magic;

(*b*) metal awls, matting or basketry needles or any other imple-ments that can be misconstrued as necrophagous cutlery;

(*c*) any charms, even defensive ones, that a suspicious neighbour would consider as belonging to a *muloi*;

(*d*) fragments of thatch or cinders taken from a neighbour's fire. These, like the hair and clippings, may be used to make sym-pathetic magic.

The eccentric, the atypical, the deformed; all are potential '*baloi*'. Women are especially liable to be suspected and Parrinder (1958. 186–187) concludes that this shows a very deep-rooted sexual an-tagonism. People living alone, the childless and the aged—in other words those living on the fringe of the group—go their own, often rather odd ways until some misfortune disturbs the harmony of the village. Midwives in a society where the infant mortality rate is so high are particularly suspect.

The gullibility of the accuser and of the ordinary individual would be amusing if the result were not so often tragic. In 1958, after a broadcast on the subject of witchcraft, the following letters, among many others, were received by the Federal Broadcasting Corporation in Lusaka:

Kabvulumvulu, listen to me,

About this witchcraft. I went to bed on June 10th and untied my shoes. When I woke up the following morning I found that my two pairs of shoes were missing. I found them outside having been gnawed by a rat. I believe that the rat was sent by a sorcerer. Yours,

Kabvulumbulu,

You there in the Broadcasting say there is no witchcraft. . . . I want to tell you we were playing football here the other day; there was an old man with a fly wisp standing opposite one goal. The teams could not score. But when one man snatched the tail from the old man, there were several goals. So, there *is* witchcraft. Stay well. (Federal Broadcasting Corporation, roneo.)

The writers were not primitive villagers. They both lived in Salisbury.

An incident similar to that described in the second letter occurred in Livingstone in 1960. The climax of a public performance of *makishi* dancing, organized by the Rhodes-Livingstone Museum, was an acrobatic dance performed at the top of a pair of poles, twenty-five to thirty feet tall, by Nalindele, one of the characters. After a number of unsuccessful attempts to climb the poles, the dancer gave up and explained to me that one of the women in the supporting chorus had 'medicine' on her hands. When she clapped she was able to prevent his climbing the poles. He refused to point out the woman for fear of involving her in a charge of witchcraft. Before the dance scheduled for the next day, however, he intended to arrange that her menstruation would occur and prevent her coming to the dance. At this second dance he performed successfully. Unfortunately, I was unable to find out whether his 'arrangements' had gone according to plan, or whether the woman suspected had merely been frightened away.

So very often misfortunes that are the result of error or clumsiness are ascribed to witchcraft. Whether or not this explanation is accepted by the rest of the village depends on the circumstances. It does, however, give the person involved an excuse other than his own fault. In the case of the pole dancer my personal view was that the fault lay with the poles that had been cut and erected by the dancer himself. The bark of the one he chose to climb was smooth. Encumbered by his costume and mask this proved too difficult. At the second dance he used the other pole, with a suitably coarse bark which afforded him a satisfactory grip. By alleging magical interference, however, he saved both his face and his reputation as a dancer.

Among the Azande, the witch is identified by divination or by an oracle, and is not required to make a detailed confession of his malpractices. In central Africa, however, the *muloi* is and usually does. From publicly recognized practising sorcerers, such statements are understandable; from the apparently innocent and harmless ordinary person they are not for, although some confessions are obtained by threats or even by force, often they appear to be voluntary, though no more credible in view of their extravagant claims. No doubt, in some cases the desire to make a false confession arises from a hunger for excitement and notoriety.[1] So often the accused is an insignificant, though once significant, member of the community. Here is an opportunity, perhaps the last, to be the focus of attention.

Field (1958 and 1960) records a number of cases where the self-confessed witch is neurotic and obsessed with the idea of guilt; 'It is mainly in retrospect at the age of involutional melancholia, that the witch looks back and feels that she has killed her children' (1958.7). On the other hand, Munday (1951.13) considers, 'It would seem that the majority of men and women over middle age have tried to use witchcraft,' in order to avenge some injury. The majority of the inhabitants of a village are probably kin. It is not practicable in such a small community for all minor disputes, insults and injuries to be made the subject of a court case and redress sought before the law. 'The only thing one can do is to bear hatred in one's heart and try to get one's own back by secret means – by using witchcraft.'

Even where a man has not tried to employ witchcraft he must often have wished bad luck on some co-villager and, should anything happen to the latter and he be accused of witchcraft, it would not be too difficult for him to believe in his own guilt. This explana-

[1] Comparable perhaps with the number of people who, in Europe, when a murder or other crime of violence has been committed, go to the police to confess.

tion would not cover the more extravagant confessions. It is feasible, however, that dreams might. Witches are reputed to work by night and to be capable of all kinds of supernatural tricks. It is possible that, lonely and unwanted, the supposed witch seeks an escape through his dreams. He realizes that throughout the village he is half-believed to be a witch and, after a few such dreams, he is sure he is.

It is difficult to decide whether Barotse witches are considered to practise in the flesh or merely in spirit. All the claims are for the former ; most of the facts, especially with regard to necrophagy, point to the latter. The dream theory, however, fits both explanations.[1] The witch sincerely believes his dreams to be reality but the material world is unchanged by his wanderings. What is more likely, therefore, than that the witch acts only in spirit. In view of the belief that witches are supposed to congregate round the rising sun, it is most unlikely that they could travel in the flesh.[2]

Melland (1923.191 and 202) suggests that witchcraft in Africa might be an old religion or fertility cult and that perhaps there is an hereditary guild of master witches. He is unable, however, to produce any evidence to support either of these theories ; neither has any subsequent writer on witchcraft in north-western Rhodesia. During the investigations no evidence suggested that witchcraft practices are in any way organized. The only possible exceptions are the feasts of the necrophagers. These, assembling at the graveside, raise the dead, divide the spoils and consume the meat, either together in the graveyard or alone in ther own homes. There appears to be no group ritual, only individual acts designed to protect each necrophager from the vengeance of his victim. All other witchcraft appears to be performed in solitude. Fertility practices were, of course, recorded but it would be difficult to prove that they were part of a cult. Again they appeared to be acts performed by individuals for their own benefit ; for example, one woman dug holes in her garden and made each of her sons urinate in them in order to improve the crops. The interesting belief was also recorded that to obtain a good crop a human body should be buried or planted in the garden at planting time. To ensure a good harvest, the corpse should be reaped with the crops and taken to the granaries. This is strikingly similar to European fertility beliefs, but it is very slender evi-

[1] I know of no cases of Bantu making use of hallucinogenic drugs.
[2] The Bantu also believe that witches can fly.

dence on which to base a theory of fertility cults and old religions. As Melland concludes 'it would seem that more evidence is required'.

Cannibalism and Necrophagy

Beliefs in the practices of cannibalism and necrophagy are widespread throughout central Africa and are indeed to be found in most parts of the continent. These beliefs are taken seriously by the local peoples and, at least in Barotseland, the consumption of human flesh is synonymous with witchcraft and the offender is straightway labelled a *muloi*.

Cannibalism has long been practised in central Africa. Hogg (1958) devotes a complete chapter to 'Cannibalism in the Congo Basin' and quotes a number of sober reports written by travellers and missionaries of this and the last century. While cannibalism was the more commonly practised, necrophagy too was observed:

The Bambala . . . regarded as special delicacies human flesh that had been buried for some days; . . . . The women of the tribe were forbidden to touch human flesh, but had found many ways of circumventing the tabu, and were particularly addicted to human flesh, extracted from graves and in an advanced stage of decomposition. (Quoting Bentley, 1900.)

In the afforested portions of north-western Rhodesia, especially among the LUNDA-LUVALE tribes,[1] it is commonly accepted that some individuals, unable to satisfy their craving for meat, may turn to human flesh. Since such individuals are usally unable through age or infirmity to hunt game, or through poverty to own livestock, and lack close kin who would be socially obliged to support them, such a belief is reasonable. The aged have long since lost their wealth to their descendants; they are entitled through tenuous kinship ties or membership of the local residence group to a few odd scraps from a slain beast; they hold no economically useful place in this group and are considered close to death. But this very proximity to death must turn their minds to the human flesh that has so often been interred before their eyes. Used in the past to reasonable supplies of meat, and dentally ill-equipped to deal with the tough scraps that now come their way, they must be only too eager to tap this supply, especially if tradition and local belief already ascribe such a practice

---

[1] Who incidentally file their teeth to sharp points, a practice often associated with cannibalism.

to them. Cannibalism as such would normally be out of the question, for it would require an active man to murder and spirit away a victim (or *vice versa*) without being discovered in the subsequent search. Usually, it would seem, the *muloi* selects and kills his victim by magic, rather than wait for a fortuitous natural death, and then, after its burial, steals the corpse for a feast. The victim is normally selected from among the kin of the *muloi*, another potential source of friction between related co-villagers.

Can one seriously accept that necrophagy is practised on a wide scale? The evidence in favour is often flimsy and basically hearsay. Nobody in recent years has been caught red-handed with his teeth sunk in a joint of human flesh, nor has any *muloi* ever been seen working at a grave. It is possible that these feasts are the products of dreams or of a vivid imagination, or that they involve the eating of the spirit of the deceased by the spirits or familiars of the witches. Indeed Delachaux (1946.45) refers to Tyivokwe (Chokwe) *baloi* as '*mangeurs d'âmes*'. On the other hand, local informants, including the suspects themselves, are quite insistent that human flesh is actually consumed and are able to convince responsible observers:

On balance, I felt at the time that there was a good deal of imagination employed in the whole business of flesh eating; but from what I have heard, I think the actual flesh was consumed.[1]

The eating of human flesh is an old point. There are several known cases of such cannibalism at Mwinilunga and Balovale. At Mwinilunga an old hag was on one occasion a few years ago found walking along carrying a human arm which she admitted to having removed from a grave and which she was proposing to eat. (White, 1948b.96.)

Kuntz (1932.137) too was satisfied that actual flesh (*chair*) is eaten and notes, 'J'ai souvent entendu de nuit, sur le cimetière proche de notre station, des bruits identiques à celui que fait l'instrument du chirurgien quand il sectionne les os et j'ai vu des tombes ouvertes et vidées.' This could be the work of hyenas though it is probable, in view of the close relationship considered to exist between *baloi* and hyenas, that local opinion would still consider it the work of *baloi*, in hyena form.

Some confessions too are not to be dismissed lightly, as for example that of the Totela woman who dug up the body of the young

[1] District Commissioner, Mankoya; personal communication, 1958. The then District Commissioner, Kalabo, held a similar view.

girl she claimed to have poisoned, only to find that it was already too decomposed to be eaten. Again, some explanation is necessary of why seventy-three people were found, during the investigations, in possession of human remains of some kind; unfortunately these were usually bones, no flesh was found. These remains must have been stolen from graves. One may accept, therefore, that flesh too can be removed.

Just as *baloi* are required to contribute a kinsman periodically to the necrophagers' feasts, so sorcerers and witchdoctors are required to kill one or more of their close relatives as part of their initiation. From these corpses certain parts, often the genitals, are taken and incorporated in the new magician's medicines and charms. He may also be required to eat selected parts of the corpse. These acts are intended to increase the powers of the magician, just as eating human flesh is supposed to increase the powers of the witch.[1] The underlying principle whereby the performance of a highly dangerous act of magic and the deliberate breaking of a serious taboo greatly increase one's magical powers and at the same time place oneself outside normal society and subject to attack by other magicians, requires no further comment here.

It may be concluded that grave-robbing still occurs in Barotseland and its environs, and that this is done either to obtain parts of the corpses for use in charms and medicines or to obtain human flesh for consumption. While few of the supposed cases of necrophagy can be considered to involve the eating of material flesh, it is fairly certain that such flesh is occasionally eaten in secret either by individuals or by small groups. Whether such people are practising a definite rite or are merely trying to augment a diet deficient in protein is difficult to decide. While group feasts appear to be attended only by witches, it is feasible that some sorcerers, having once or twice indulged in necrophagy, may find the practice to their taste and allow it to develop into a habit.

Selection and Training of the muloi

The information available on the selection, initiation and training of *baloi* is regrettably scant. Witches would appear to be initiated by their mother or by another older relative, being given or inheriting familiars and being introduced to necrophagy either by a trick, 'She had been given a handful of monkey nuts to eat. She had eaten them

---

[1] This is perhaps analogous to the ritual murders of the Basuto.

and next day the donor had said that she had eaten human flesh,'[1] or quite openly :

She was hoeing in her garden many years ago when she heard voices. On going to look she saw her mother and some other women sitting round a fire and cutting up a baby which they cooked. She was discovered by them and told that as she knew their secret she must become one of them. She was then given a cinder to swallow and a bundle of sticks of medicine and a bodkin. Later she partook of many such feasts and herself killed one of her own babies and contributed it to a feast. (White, 1948b.96.)

How the aspirant sorcerer begins his career is a matter for conjecture. No doubt he apprentices himself to a known sorcerer for a fee, but just how he makes the first approach is not clear. Local belief has it that to consult a sorcerer is to indicate a desire to learn sorcery and perhaps this is the initial step. The apprentice may, as happens in more reputable professions, be a member of the sorcerer's family or kin and is, therefore, taught at a reduced or nominal fee. He may have become an aspirant either with a definite motive (for example, revenge) in mind or because he is truly keen on the profession. However he begins, he must soon realize he is on a treadmill which, irrespective of his personal wishes, compels him to improve his knowledge to save his life.

EQUIPMENT AND METHODS

Broadly speaking, the weapons employed by the *muloi* may be separated into three groups, each of which is discussed separately below. Many of these weapons are employed too by witchdoctors, while familiars are also possessed by diviners. In this chapter, attention is restricted to the use made of them by *baloi*.

FAMILIARS

The definition of a familiar as an attendant is inadequate in considering Barotse familiars and, therefore, in this paper the term is used in the sense of agents or animated weapons capable of seeking out the victim and of carrying out the task assigned by their master. Such agents may receive specific rewards or may even be entitled to be given regular opportunities of killing. They do not, however, select their own victims nor do they act independently of their master, unless he fails to keep the agreement he has made with them.

[1] District Commissioner, Mankoya; personal communication, 1958.

Fig. 2. Figures representing familiar spirits (i)

a. Female figure   c. Mask with sisal beard
b. Female figure   d. Seated figure; no sexual features
                             e. Luvale *kaponya* stylized figure

28

These familiars are possessed by male *baloi*. Most of the reputed *baloi* arrested were female and it is, therefore, surprising, especially in view of White's (1948b.84)[1] statement, '*ndumba* . . . figure in three-quarters of the accusations of witchcraft in the northwest. Among the Lwena and Luchazi particularly *ndumba* and *uloji* (*baloi*) are almost synonymous,' that at no time were *tuyebela* or *vandumba*, familiars employed by female *baloi*, mentioned.

Turner (1957.144–145) describes *tuyebela*, synonymous with *vandumba*, as follows:

variable forms of little men with reversed feet, hyenas, jackals. They are believed to be inherited matrilineally and to make demands on their owners to kill junior relatives. They may be refused three times but after that, however hard the owner (*nkaka*) may plead, they kill their chosen victim. When the owner of *tuyebela* dies, they seek out one of her close kin, it may be a daughter or uterine sister, and attach themselves to her whether she desires them or not. Their victims are the husbands or junior matrilineal kin of their owners. If a husband is killed his ghost becomes what is known as a *kahwehwi*, and leads the band of *tuyebela*. He is more powerful than they, and may only be gainsaid once. *Tuyebela* are exceptionally active if their owner has a grudge (*chitela*) against someone, when they are liable to take instant action against him without asking their owner.

Of those familiars that were noted, there appear to be various types, most of which are represented in real life by an inanimate symbol or figure, often of carved wood (Figs. 2, 3 and 4). This is kept by the master.

Familiars in Human Shape

These familiars—variously called *likishi, mwanankishi, kanenga, litotola, kaponya, nameya* or *kanameya*, are all shades (*silumba*, pl. *balumba*) stolen from the newly deceased. The *muloi* raises the corpse by magic from the grave, restores it to life, and then ceremonially kills it again.[2] This process leaves him in possession of the desired shade and the corpse is returned to the grave. The *muloi* usually provides himself with a carved figure to represent the shade.

While these familiars are of LUNDA-LUVALE origin, their acceptance by neighbouring tribes has been such that they are now fairly

[1] White notes that the familiars of the former are not inherited, but that those (*vandumba*) of the latter are.

[2] According to Kuntz (1932.137), the corpse itself does not appear; only the shade is raised. There is, therefore, no need for a second death.

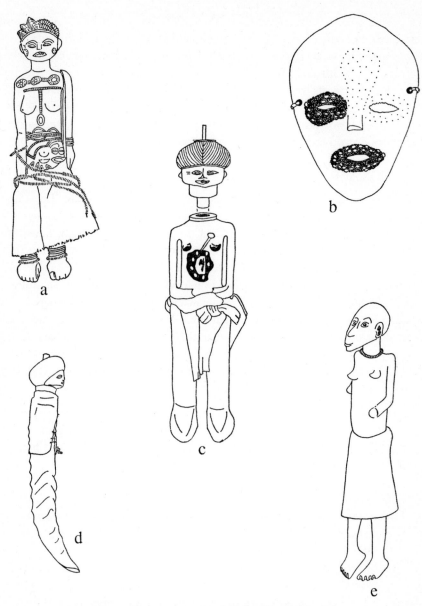

Fig. 3. Figures representing familiar spirits (ii)

a. Chokwe *likishi* female figure, with movable left arm
b. Shanjo *likishi* mask; lucky beans are impressed in the beeswax round the mouth and right eye; the dotted lines indicate areas formerly also covered with beeswax
c. Female figure with detachable head; large nail driven between breasts and fragment of glass set in beeswax below
d. Mbunda divining horn with carved wooden head inserted; the point of the horn is heavily worn through use
e. Female figure

extensively 'employed' throughout Barotseland. Despite their different names, the figures representing these familiars have much the same features, and the spirits themselves behave in much the same way.

Unlike its European counterpart, the Barotse familiar travels on foot in search of its victim. Should anybody have the misfortune to encounter it in its nocturnal travels, the meeting is fatal for him. It would appear that the familiar is not invisible and that it resembles the inanimate figure which symbolizes it during the hours of daylight. Whether it is this figure that is actually animated, as some informants suggest, or whether it is merely a shelter for the spirit which is conjured up independently of it, is difficult to say, though the fact that the figure contains in its body the essential medicines and charms would indicate that the former is more likely. If this is so, then the animated figure is probably the same size as the doll and not of full human proportions. Some informants describe the figures as having detachable heads (Fig. 3(c)) to enable the spirit to enter and return at the will of the master, but few of the figures actually collected possessed this refinement.

Whilst most *baloi* direct the attentions of their familiars against specific victims, it would seem that witchdoctors allow theirs more freedom and, since witchdoctors and sorcerers often make use of the same weapons, one finds familiars, such as *likishi* or *kanenga*, which actually seek out or even indicate witches before killing them.

The magical weapon which is most commonly used by familiars, whether they be employed by *baloi* or by witchdoctors, is a small knife. This is usually carried in the left hand. Strangely enough, whilst no essential detail is spared in the construction of figures, no instance has come to light of any one of them being armed with such a knife. Yet it is so frequently mentioned, both in the records and by informants, as an indispensable part of their equipment. Some figures also have small horns set in the crown of the head. One Luvale *likishi*, instead of using a knife to despatch its victim, merely took out the horn when in his presence. No further information is available as to what would cause the actual death. Perhaps the removal of the horn permitted the exit of the familiar or, more probably, the capture and imprisonment of the spirit of the victim. Another method is for a medicated human skull to be placed on the head of a *mwanankishi* figure if death is desired; this was only recorded on one occasion. Yet another is to place a *likishi* figure in the

Fig. 4. Figures representing familiar spirits (iii); *linkalankala*

a. Badly worn figure carrying a hoe or axe on the left shoulder
b. A most unusual figure consisting of a length of reed, covered by a sleeve of twisted
bark strip, resembling crochet work. The hair is human (African) and the face is of
beeswax with lucky beans impressed for eyes. The cape and skirt are of strips of bark
c. Mashi *likishi* figure; the detachable mask is of cloth sewn to a frame of small sticks and
the beard is of sisal. The mask is set on a wooden stem, wrapped with snake skin. Two
sikuyeti sticks are attached
d. *Linkalankala*

path of the victim so as to bewitch him. One figure so used was somewhat peculiar in that it was made from a ram's horn and was covered by a glove.

Finally, I would like to quote an extract from a Mongu case record involving the possession of a *nameya* figure. While no evidence is available as to the use to which this was put, the peculiar behaviour of the owner makes one strongly suspect the practice of sorcery: 'When he (a Totela) sleeps with his wife he inserts his tongue into her vagina and also removes blood from between her breasts and prepares medicines to wash her (the *nameya* figure) . . . all these unnatural acts . . . he did regularly to his former wives. . . .' This may be merely a spiteful accusation on the part of the wife or, even if true, aberrant sexual behaviour. Yet there is a certain similarity to the ritual associated with the creation of an *ilomba*. Could the accused have been attempting to create a familiar?

Muhole

The *muhole* sorcerer obtains his familiars in a different fashion. He steals a living human victim by whistling, according to an Nkoya informant, on a magic horn set in the butt of his flyswitch. The victim cannot resist the call and is spirited away into the bush. The flyswitch now takes on human form and goes to the village where it impersonates the victim. After a few days the simulacrum 'sickens', 'dies', is buried by the relatives and retrieved at leisure by its owner. The victim has not been missed from the village and may either be kept as an actual slave, killed to provide flesh for a feast or turned into a familiar.

During the investigations, a case of *muhole* theft was brought to the notice of the District Commissioner, Kalabo. A woman claimed that when she was a young girl she was stolen by a *muhole* sorcerer and was duly replaced by his flyswitch. Whilst hidden in the bush she heard her relatives wailing at her own funeral. Now, as a grown woman, she had returned from Angola whither she had been taken, and had come to her old village where she was recognized and identified by one of the villagers.

A similar case was noted in 1961 in the same district under the name of *mutukule* :[1]

In Liondo village . . . a woman was presented to me who was said to have been raised from the dead. She 'died' in 1925 and many of the villagers (includ-

[1] Kalabo district files, 1961.

33

ing the Senior District Messenger who accompanied me on this tour) say they remember her death and subsequent burial. The woman, her name is Kutemba, says that one day she was accosted near the village by two men who were strangers to her. They held her down and kept her outside the village. They then mixed some medicine in a cowhorn which they then wrapped in a blanket and took into the village saying that Kutemba's dead body was contained in it. To all present it appeared to be Kutemba's body and so they proceeded to bury the blanket containing the cowhorn (which was later recovered by the owners) with the traditional mourning, etc. The woman says that she watched the ceremony, which she says she found extremely agonizing, but to the people she seemed to be invisible. She was eventually taken to Angola by the men where she worked as their servant. After a number of years (one of the men) died and his village was scattered and Kutemba returned with (his) son to near Liumba Hill Mission and then went north to live in Balovale District. Her relatives in Liondo village (who are Luvale) heard that she was there and within the last few months brought her back.

Melland (1923.214–218) records Kaonde beliefs in the practice of *uhori (muhole)*, though he gives the word the wider meaning of the 'power of invisibility'. White (1948b.101) derives the noun, *uholi*, from the verb, *hola*, 'to spirit away'. His description of the practice varies little from that of Melland and would appear to have been based upon it.

Animal and Non-Human Familiars

One of the most important of these is *linkalankala* (Fig. 4(d)), a small tortoise or turtle shell filled with a medicine composed of the ash of charred roots mixed with fat. From the front end of the tortoise the point of a small knife-blade protrudes, the rest being buried in the medicine.[1] This is again a LUNDA-LUVALE weapon, though nowadays it is employed by other tribes in the Protectorate.

Linkalankala acts in much the same way as those familiars already described. It moves by night through the village and attacks its victim with the knife. In some instances the knife is merely pointed at the victim, thereby bewitching him. White (1948b.101) notes that *nkala* also lives in rivers and is supposed to resemble a large crab with big claws and nose-like projections. Singleton-Fisher (1949. 20–21) distinguishes between *kalankata* :

---

[1] It may also consist of a charmed bottle of water, though no specimen has been observed by the writer.

the shell of a very large snail (*Acontias*). . . . This shell is considered to be capable of becoming a very powerful weapon in magical warfare when properly treated by the witch-doctor. The Lunda say that it will turn into a magical snail and will carry a knife at night and crawl to the intended victim's hut and cut his throat. A severe attack of laryngitis or any pain in the throat might be attributed to this familiar;

and *nkala* the crab :

(This) is considered even more deadly. An empty crab shell is taken to the witch-doctor and filled by him with the necessary charms. It is not clear exactly what is done with the object after this, but the result is that a powerful spirit crab takes up its abode in the river at the crossing nearest to the home of its owner. This crab reaches out its long claws and grabs the shadow (*mwevulu*, also used for the soul) of its intended victim as he crosses the river. It seems that this practice is rarely used and so the people are consequently rather vague as to the symptoms produced by anybody 'eaten' by a crab. Death is generally the final result.

Kaututumbwa is a ball of cow-dung into which the teeth of a spring hare are embedded. The ball is further studded with red and black lucky beans (*Abrus precatorius*) which indicate its evil nature. Although the teeth are believed to pull out the throat of the victim, it is unlikely that a visible wound results from such a nocturnal attack. *Kaututumbwa* is referred to in only one case; the owner was an Mbunda.

Another member of the group, the name of which was unfortunately not recorded, is a medicated tortoise shell which has inserted, in place of the knife blade, two 'magic' horns. The tortoise moves through the village at night and leads the sorcerer to the victim it selects. The actual killing is left to the sorcerer.

Ilomba

The best known of all central African familiars, and the only one on which there is much literature, is the *ilomba*, otherwise known as *lilombamema* or, by the Kaonde, *mulombe*.[1] This has a distribution which extends far beyond the borders of Barotseland. No doubt it is also known in contiguous parts of Angola, particularly in a northerly and north-westerly direction.

It is interesting how the descriptions of Melland, writing in 1923

---

[1] Melland also notes other Kaonde names, *mulolo* and *sung'unyi* (archaic), for this creature.

of the Kaonde, of White, writing in 1948b of the tribes of Balovale and Mwinilunga districts, of Singleton-Fisher, writing in 1949 of the inhabitants of the southern Congo, and of Turner, writing in 1957 of the Ndembu of Mwinilunga as observed beteeen 1950 and 1954, resemble very closely not only each other but also the notes made in 1957 by the magistrates at Sesheke and Mongu. When one remembers that the informants of these magistrates had had no access to the written accounts, had probably never heard of their authors, and were unlikely, especially in Sesheke district, to have visited or lived in the districts north and east of the Protectorate, this resemblance is remarkable.

The *ilomba* is a water-snake familiar which is created by a sorcerer either for himself or for a client. The body of the creature is that of a snake, but the head is human in form and closely resembles the head of its owner. Melland states that even the ornaments worn by the owner are duplicated on the *ilomba*. Unlike the familiars described above, the *ilomba* and for that matter all familiars of this group, are so closely linked to their owners that their destruction must result in the death of the latter.

The following account of how an Nkoya created his *ilomba* is taken from case records but differs only in slight details from that given by White. Melland's account shows greater differences in that he infers that the *ilomba* was created before the eyes of the client by the sorcerer (witchdoctor).

He took blood from his back, chest and forehead and took his severed finger nails, and medicine from forest roots and mixed them up and put it all in Chamba Pan. A similar action was taken twice daily for some days at the end of which time the snake was beginning to grow. The snake is used for magical purposes but it will not kill as the accused will remove its teeth or he says he will do so. The snake will be able to cause death after five years.

Another Nkoya *ilomba* is described as follows: 'This one is the length of a forearm . . . has caused five deaths. It is a normal snake but has the face of its owner . . . seen only by victims. It wanted blood.'

The final sentence of the second quotation, whilst not strictly accurate, gives the key to the *ilomba*/sorcerer relationship. The *ilomba* demands victims. It is created from blood and is fed in infancy on milk and eggs. Soon it demands meat—a foetus, then a babe and finally an adult. After each killing, when it feasts off the spirit not the blood of the victim, it increases in size and strength. One Mwenyi informant suggested that it grows an extra head for each person killed, but this is an unconfirmed statement and one may accept the more usual belief that it merely increases in size. One interesting use by a Lozi sorcerer of his *ilomba* was not only the killing of victims, the last of which was his own granddaughter, but also the exhumation of the corpses for his own consumption.

The following account, recorded at Mankoya, provides some additional data of interest.

He had approached a well-known purveyor of medicine some years ago for some medicine to help him in hunting. In return for twelve hand-made hoes given by the subject to the purveyor, he had received some medicine in powder form. This medicine he was told to place in the hollow of a tree and to water it. He did this and was horrified to find later that it had turned into a snake. The snake chose to live in the river, and he found that it could talk. At first the snake was content to live on chickens. It then turned its attention to dogs and small livestock. Finally the snake demanded that its owner should direct it to specified human beings. The owner was now in a quandary. He knew that the snake possessed his soul, and that if it was not satisfied, he would die. The snake would come to him for instructions every two or three months and the owner was obliged to send it to suck the blood of his relatives and to kill them. Nor could he kill the snake because he would die. The owner stated that all the houses of the village were interconnected by tunnels through which the snake would travel.[1]

Singleton-Fisher (1949.21–22) was also informed, 'The owner digs a tunnel from his hut to the stream. The *ilomba* comes up the tunnel at night to converse with its owner.' He further records that in the Kalene Hill (Mwinilunga) area:

A Lunda friend dug up the 'seed' of an *ilomba* in his garden near the head of a small stream. This he brought to me in great excitement, surrounded by a crowd of shouting, greatly agitated men. The seed consisted of a bushbuck horn filled with charms embedded into grease. This I was told was to represent the main body of the *ilomba*. In the opening of the horn, stuck into the mass of grease and charms was a duiker horn filled with the same mixture of charms and grease, into which was pushed a brass cartridge case. This they said was the head of the *ilomba* and the cartridge case was put in to make it invulnerable. The Africans now showed they had no fear whatsoever of the charm. They

---

[1] District Commissioner, Mankoya; personal communication, 1958.

37

argued that it could do them no harm unless it came to life and that it could only do so when buried in the ground sufficiently near to the head of a stream. They explained, with much laughter, that this charm was obviously a dud and that the witchdoctor, who had made it and had probably collected a large fee, was no doubt a cheat. If the charm, the seed of the *ilomba*, had been a good one, a worm would have come out of it which would have wriggled its way down to the stream and have changed rapidly into an invisible serpent. The serpent would take up its abode at the crossing and swallow the shadows of its owner's enemies and grow several hundred yards in length for each shadow swallowed. Those who had their shadows swallowed would become violently ill, vomit sand and die. . . .

Finally the *ilomba*'s demands become so exorbitant . . . that the owner will commit suicide rather than accede to them. Lundas are often seen wearing round their necks fish hooks or the very sharp horn of the white-backed duiker to prevent the *ilomba* swallowing them.

An alternative fate for the owner of the *ilomba* is its discovery by a witchdoctor who then shoots it with a *wuta wawufuku* (*kaliloze* gun, see Chapter II), thereby killing the *muloi*.

On the other animal spirits of this type mentioned by White (1948b.101–102) and Singleton-Fisher (1949.20–22), *nzovu* (elephant) and *nguvu* (hippopotamus), no data was gathered during the investigations. This tends to confirm White's opinion that belief in them is on the wane.

There are a number of instances of the use of wild animals as familiars, a practice formerly common in Europe. Thus a Luvale diviner/doctor, curing a patient in Sesheke of sickness caused by witchcraft, afterwards discovered nearby the corpse of a jackal. This he considered to be a defeated familiar. Another instance noted in Mankoya was of 'an evil spirit in the form of a lizard only a few inches long'. So like the European type is this sort of familiar that, if it were not for the vernacular terms, the following translated quotation might belong not to twentieth-century Africa but to seventeenth-century England. It is, in fact, an extract from a letter written or rather dictated by a notorious Totela witchdoctor, living in Sesheke, and sent to his clients :

We have seen your Mukubesa (villager) has seven spirits, the eighth is Munalula. He has got *Kakundukundu* (whirlwind) and *Nyunywani* (bird) they are in his house. Manyando (another villager) has eight spirits and also Kekelwa is with him, he has Dama Wakumelo's medicine. He is a bad man in his village;

he should not be allowed to transfer them to anyone. Lutangu's came from his parents.

From the last two sentences one may deduce that such familiars are transferable, just as Melland (1923.207) states the *ilomba* is among the Kaonde. Since this is a letter, not a confession, and comes from an already notorious witchdoctor, whose first conviction dates from 1917, one may accept it as a reliable source. This is fortunate, for rarely otherwise is there any information on this type of familiar.

Lycanthropy or shape-shifting, the temporary adoption of an animal form, also occurs among the Barotse.[1] The jackal mentioned above may possibly have been such a creature, and there are other references to this practice.

Lane Poole (ms.) notes the close association believed by the Nsenga to exist between the *muloi*/necrophager and the hyena. Kuntz (1932.127–129) also records the use of lions and hyenas in the practice of shape-shifting and the use of owls and nightjars as familiars. It would appear that creatures of the night, that are dangerous to man, or that creep or crawl are especially suited to the purposes of the *muloi*.

The death of the *muloi* is obtained by killing the creature containing his spirit. Kuntz mentions this with reference to lion-men. The same method is employed by *sikuyeti* doctors who set a small trap and, by cutting off the head of the snared bird or animal, kill the *muloi*.

SIPOSO

Siposo, the projection of magic in the form of an invisible missile, has been encountered even more frequently during the investigations than have familiars. This has been partly because of its association, especially during 1956 in Kalabo, with *kaliloze* guns, and partly because of the needle charm which has been so widely and eagerly accepted by the local peoples as a defence against *siposo* or, in some cases, as an aid to its projection.

The noun, *siposo*, 'something that is thrown or sent', is derived from the Lozi verb, *kuposa*, 'to throw'. While the verb may be used quite freely wherever the act of throwing needs to be expressed, the noun is only employed in connection with magic. This fact is widely known and the noun as widely employed, but not until Symon

---

[1] See also Chapter VI. The *Sitondo*.

(roneo)[1] described *siposo* as an actual ailment, did it occur in the literature on medico/magical practices. Lawrance[2] considers that the needle charm was first heard of in or about 1928, from people coming back from Wankie, in connection with *siposo* killings. Yet, if *siposo* was known as long ago as this, it would be reasonable to expect, assuming it had then something of its present importance, that Gluckman, Melland, Turner or White would have mentioned it.[3] It may be concluded that *siposo* is a L U Y A N A concept, possibly introduced from the south, which has only recently been accepted by the L U N D A-L U V A L E.

The importance of the needle charm as a *siposo* defence is based on the homoeopathic assumption that like affects like. Since the *siposo* missile is most often an invisible needle, though it may also be a nail or a fly, a needle charm is the most reliable defence. Singleton-Fisher (1949.20) notes that sharp chest pains in pneumonia cases are usually considered to be wounds caused by a *kaliloze* gun.

A *siposo* missile, of which sorcerers and also rain doctors are very fond, is lightning,[4] and many of those who have been found wearing needle charms have strongly asserted their fears of this form of attack. Just how the homoeopathic or sympathetic principle applies in this case is not clear. Probably the wearer, as so often happens in such matters, makes too great an assumption and likens the sharp prick of a needle to the stab of a fork of lightning.

A Luvale sorcerer was found to possess, among other sinister apparatus, a very unusual *siposo* weapon called *sikulukulu*, a padlock studded with lucky beans; this lock when closed cuts off the life of the victim, just as did the shears of Atropos.

It is to be emphasized that the mere possession of a needle as a protective charm does not enable the wearer to project *siposo*. Projection is a highly skilled and dangerous affair for the witchdoctor or sorcerer who employs it; should the attack be parried, the missile returns to harm the sender. He must, therefore, wear needle charms,

---

[1] *Siposo* as an ailment is discussed in Chapter III.

[2] Senanga files, 1957. Needle charms are discussed in Chapter III.

[3] Gluckman knew the noun though he did not write about it; personal communication, 1959. Melland (1923) does not even mention the projection of magic. Turner did not encounter the term during his field-work among the Ndembu; personal communication, 1959. White (1948b.100) discusses the projection of magic but makes no mention of the term *siposo*.

[4] Melland (1923.155) states that the Kaonde believe Lesa, the Creator, 'shows his power by thunder and lightning – which latter occasionally kills people,' but that they have no other belief or superstition about either of these two phenomena.

or perhaps *ngoba* beads, as a defence in case of failure. The *ngoba*, which are an assortment of actual Venetian and other beads and carved pieces of root, are usually worn as a bracelet (Fig. 6(a), (b) and (c)) and are only to be found in the possession of a *siposo* expert. Their possession is proof positive of deep knowledge of, and great skill in *siposo* matters. The owner may be either a sorcerer or witch-doctor.

DIRECT ATTACK

Direct attack, as opposed to a *siposo* attack, requires the contact or close proximity of the weapon used to the body of the victim. No familiar spirit acts for the sorcerer; he is his own agent. The methods employed are varied, but may be said to fall under some three heads—poison, charms and *taka*.

Poisons (*mabela*)

The use here of the term, 'poisoning', is merely a convenient way of describing a particular type of activity on the part of a sorcerer, and refers to the introduction or attempted introduction of any poisonous or supposedly poisonous powder or similar substance into the stomach, lungs or flesh of the victim with the object of causing his death or illness.

The simplest and most effective way of administering poison to a victim is orally. A beer drink, where the poison, usually in powder form or in solution, may be slipped into food or drink, is a good occasion for the attack, the poison being secreted in the hand or perhaps under a fingernail. Some sorcerers, however, like some criminals in European society, are not content to use these straightforward methods. One administered poison by slipping into the hut of the sleeping victim and blowing the powdered poison over the whole of his body, paying particular attention to the mouth. Others restrict their attention, during such nocturnal visits, to the mouth only and ignore the rest of the body.[1] Poison may also be introduced subcutaneously in the following manner, as described by a Luchazi sorcerer:

A piece of iron (*mukumbo*) was buried in a path which the victim frequented. The point was anointed with lime (*pepa*) and with a poison made from *ka-shiamusongo* leaves. The victim trod thereon and two days later died. In the

[1] District Commissioner, Mankoya; personal communication, 1958.

41

intervening period his chest is said to have swelled and a boil to have appeared on his neck.

Another method, as explained by a sorceress in Kalabo, is to visit the victim when sick and, under the pretence of commiserating with him, to prick his body with a necrophager's fork (Fig. 1(e) and (g)) or with a medicated needle set in a ball of beeswax (Fig. 1(j)). The patient's condition deteriorates rapidly and he dies. A similar result can be obtained by the sorcerer anointing his body with a mixture of powdered lime and human fat, and then visiting the patient. As he walks towards the patient the poison takes effect.[1]

Most of the poisons, either actual or magical, used in this part of central Africa have a vegetable base. Leaves, and especially roots of trees and shrubs, are the parts most commonly employed, just as they are in the preparation of medicines to treat ordinary sickness. Some trees or shrubs, such as *mubako* (*Erythrophloeum africanum*)[2] have been analysed and found to be poisonous. Others, such as *mulya-shinji* (*Capparis tomentosa*), were, until recently, in doubt. There are many reputed poisons—for example, those obtained from *mutulo-muko* roots,[3] from *mankonde* grass, from *kashiamusongo* leaves, and the *liyaya* and the *munyonga* (*Ekebergia meyeri*) trees, but in the absence of analyses or of reliable proof, and even in many cases of botanical identification, their efficacy remains in doubt.

Where the poison has a vegetable base it may not be easy, in an autopsy, to identify it. The news of the death does not filter through to the boma for at least many hours, and the corpse must then be brought to the hospital or to the boma. By this time the poison, if it exists, has had ample time to disappear without trace. Poisons which have a non-vegetable base are much more easily identified. Unfortunately, or perhaps fortunately depending upon the viewpoint, such common modern poisons as strychnine and arsenic have not so far been used, while the only non-vegetable poison recorded is that which an aspiring poisoner was found diligently preparing in a mortar. The ingredients were a blue-headed tree lizard (*Agama atricollis*)

[1] This is only a poison in the magical sense. There is also an element of sympathetic magic involved, for the fat would be taken from a corpse. The use, by the Kalabo sorcerers, of a necrophager's fork is perhaps also dependent on sympathetic magic.

[2] Another of the species, *E. guineense*, provides the poison widely used as an ordeal poison by witchdoctors (Fanshawe and Hough, 1960).

[3] Fragments of wood, taken from a stretcher used to carry a corpse to its grave, are pounded together with the roots. The use of this material with its implication of sympathetic magic is frequently met with, not only in Africa, but also in many other parts of the world.

and glass pounded up together. Whether the former or the latter was considered the lethal ingredient is unknown. Similarly, it is a matter for conjecture whether this poison has any connection with *siku* sickness which is believed to result from a blue-headed tree lizard being present in the stomach.

Charms[1]

A belief in charms as magical weapons is widely held throughout central Africa. One of the commonest ways in which they are employed is by placing them on or over, or burying them in a path frequented by the intended victim. A favourite device used in this way is a medicated tortoise shell, a 'magic tortoise'. The poisoned iron point described earlier could be considered as belonging to this group. Charms may also be hidden under the threshold of a door or gate, or even hung or laid in full view on top. The object of these attacks is to cause death, misfortune or the aborting of pregnant women.[2]

Only a few charms actually come into physical contact with the victims. The power of each of the remainder has a very limited range and requires the close proximity of the victim to have any effect.

Taka

This method involves a nocturnal visit by the *muloi* to the bedside of his victim. On arrival, he places a hollow reed (*taka*) in the mouth of his victim and sucks out either his breath or his spirit, it is not clear which. White (1948b.84) refers to *vandumba* familiars sucking out the breath,[3] keeping it in a reed and blowing it back into the corpse after burial and subsequent resurrection, in order to create an *ndumba*. There is also the practice of inserting a reed through a hole in the wall of the house, and exhaling *les émanations du mort* (Kuntz, 1932.137). Some necrophagers are said to blow through a reed into the grave to resurrect the corpse.

The inhabitants of Barotseland, in common with all Bantu-speaking peoples possess a belief in the efficacy of sympathetic magic.

---

[1] Defined as 'objects invested with magical power' (Royal Anthropological Institute, 1951.188).

[2] An aborted foetus or stillborn child is often used for magical preparations and practices. For example, an *ilomba* requires such flesh as food during the early stages of its existence.

[3] This may take place while the victim is talking. The reed is plugged at both ends. District Commissioner, Mankoya; personal communication, 1958.

Many of the methods that have been described in this chapter rely, to some extent, on this principle. Fragments of a funeral bier or of the corpse itself, hair and nail clippings, excreta, wisps of thatch or cinders, all are the raw material from which a sorcerer prepares his charms or with which he directs his attack. They also form the basis of many defensive charms and of love charms but, should anybody be found gathering them or interfering with a neighbour's fire or house thatch, he would very likely be suspected of sorcery. Such suspicions are difficult to allay and are liable to be revived at some future date.

NECROPHAGY

The methods employed by *baloi* to kill their victims have already been discussed. It is only necessary here, therefore, to describe the sequence of events beginning with the exhumation of the corpse. This is done at night and fairly soon after the day of the burial, despite the dangers of suspicious relatives. One Totela woman, who delayed for seven days, found the corpse so decomposed that she reburied it without further ado. Others, with more audacity, steal the corpse on the night following the burial, or on subsequent nights. *Baloi* usually work as a group for the exhumation, although only one of their number is responsible for the death of the victim. Each member of the group is required to provide human flesh in his turn. Most, if accounts are to be believed, find it expedient to provide one of their relatives rather than a stranger. On learning of the success of his attack, the *muloi* responsible calls up his or her colleagues and they prepare for the exhumation. According to one account of such an exhumation :

The *muloi* sits on the grave and blows down a reed filled with medicine and inserted into the soil.[1] A small hole appears in the soil and then first a leg and later a hand rise up from the grave. When the body comes into view the required parts are cut off and the remainder returns to the grave of its own accord after the chest has been smeared with a mixture of powdered medicine and human fat. Some of this mixture is also blown on to the grave. The surface of the grave is little disturbed.

No digging tools are used, and the total equipment of the *muloi*/necrophager appears to be limited to an axe and a knife for cutting up

---

[1] According to Kuntz (1932.137) the method is to knock three times on the grave.

Barotse river scene: royal barge and canoes

The royal barge (Nalikwando) paddled by Lozi *indunas* on the occasion of the visit of Her Majesty Queen Elizabeth, the Queen Mother, to Mongu, 1961

the body, a dancing hoe, culinary utensils, poisons and defensive charms (Fig. 1).

The object of the exhumation is said usually to be to obtain flesh for consumption. Sometimes, however, it is to obtain particular portions, notably the genital organs, for use in some ritual or for inclusion in a medicine.[1] In such cases the corpse is returned to the grave almost intact; normally, only the bones and the unwanted flesh are returned. Even the skull is taken, for the more of these a *muloi* possesses, the greater are his magical powers.

A detailed account by a Lozi woman of the cutting up of the corpse[2] after exhumation was recorded at Mongu. She claimed to have killed the victim, her granddaughter, by means of a *lilombamema*, and to have exhumed the body the night following its interment:

The body of Sifekiso, who was a girl who had just reached puberty, was stripped (of burial mats and blankets). The accused and companions then cut up the body with *mameko* knives, making a circular cut round the stomach to allow access to the entrails which were divided between the two women. The accused had the heart and the lungs, and the liver was divided as were the kidneys. The private parts of Sifekiso were divided as were the breasts. As regards the non-delicacies the accused took the upper portion of the body and her companion the rump and thighs. The accused and companion brought fire and clay pots with water to the graveyard and cooked the meat in the pots and then ate it. That which could not be eaten up that night was hung and dried on trees near the graveyard and this was eaten over the four successive nights. The bones were buried again in the grave.

The exhumation and division of the corpse are accompanied by dancing and celebration; indeed one accused appears to have obtained her share of the flesh solely by her dancing, and not to have been required to provide a corpse herself. Various informants also state that the flesh may be bought and sold for money.

The actual consumption of the flesh appears to be, magically, the most perilous part of the whole process. Whether the *baloi* feast together, as in the case of Sifekiso, or whether they go off to their own homes to eat in privacy, they must take certain precautions to safe-

---

[1] i.e. sorcery and not true necrophagy.

[2] Squabbling and complaints of unfair sharing seem to be frequent. One old woman even took her complaint to the District Commissioner. Turner (1957.151) notes, 'Old women . . . are constantly grumbling about lack of meat, and in a society with a lively belief in the necrophagous practices of witches, this is highly suspicious behaviour.'

guard themselves.[1] To begin with, it is dangerous to handle the meat with the fingers, for it taints them with a peculiar smell discernible by a diviner or witchdoctor.[2] The *muloi* uses, therefore, a single-pronged fork (Fig. 1(e) and (g)),[3] termed *lutabo* (needle) or *woyo* (spear). To prevent the spirit of the victim haunting him, he must circle the fork around his head and ensure that drops of the stew do not fall on his body. Some say that he would suffer from serious sores on those places where the liquid falls. Similarly, he must possess a charm or medicine to prevent his being poisoned by the poison used on the victim, or against contracting the fatal illness of the latter. His problems are increased by the efforts of the witchdoctor who, when seeking the cause of death, may so bewitch the corpse that any person or animal endeavouring to eat it will die. He may also rub a poison, in powder form, into various cuts on the body.

The meat is prepared in what appears to be normal ways. There is some suggestion that various powders are used as relishes to accompany the meal and that others are used as aids to digestion, but these have not as yet been identified.[4] Boiling and broiling are common and that which is not consumed immediately is set aside and dried, later to be roasted or grilled. The supply lasts for perhaps some ten days, though there is little data on this point.

The fat is also collected, either from the marrow bones or by boiling down the flesh, and used for a variety of purposes, the most common of which is the anointing of the body of the *muloi* in place of animal or vegetable fats. The fork may also be dipped in the fat before impaling a piece of meat, especially when the flesh is considered too lean. Flesh and fat from a corpse are considered most potent, and many *baloi* are said to keep a small pot or bottle of such materials in with their weapons. European and albino hair are also considered to be of magical importance. One finds a comparable belief in the potency of human remains in most parts of the world, and even among the Eskimo, 'The whalers are said to have killed people secretly and boiled up their fat to make poison.' (Birket-Smith, 1959.85.)

The genitals of both male and female victims seem to be much de-

---

[1] Surprisingly enough none of the supposed necrophagers arrested are recorded as wearing needle charms.

[2] Another way in which a necrophager may be identified is by repeated coughing; this is believed to be an indication that he has eaten human flesh.

[3] This is often a length of bicycle spoke sharpened at the end. The word coined, one gathers by the Africans themselves, as the name for this instrument is 'spork'.

[4] District Commissioner, Mankoya; personal communication, 1958.

sired and are considered able, especially in sorcery, to strengthen magical powers. They are also considered most valuable agriculturally for improving the crops and for ensuring a good harvest. Nails and hair may be taken from a corpse and, mixed with medicines, used for this purpose. Finally, there is the belief, discussed earlier, that to ensure good crops a body should be planted; to ensure a good harvest and that the grain will stay safe in the granaries, the body should, at reaping time, also be reaped.

In this chapter, beliefs in sorcery and witchcraft and the practices and devices ascribed to the *muloi* have been discussed in some detail. While these beliefs are in themselves of considerable ethnographic interest, one must not forget their importance to the actual people who hold them. For the African villager, witchcraft is a very serious matter. The weird and mythical spirits here described are for him very real, while the malevolent powers of *baloi* are an ever-present menace against which he must always be on his guard. His fears are latent, but rise swiftly to the surface when sickness or misfortune afflicts him, or indeed when anything mysterious or inexplicable occurs. His neighbours and relatives are his friends and constant companions and he turns to them for help whenever he is in need. Yet, at the same time, he knows that they contain his potential enemies, for *baloi* attack those near to them. When, therefore, a crisis occurs in a village and witchcraft is suspected, tension mounts and people fear and suspect each other, even their wives and close kin. This tension is relieved by the identification of the offending *muloi*. If feelings run high, as they apparently did in Mankoya in 1958, the latter may well be roughly handled, for he is a material object on which all these repressed fears of the unknown may be vented.

Witchcraft, or rather belief in witchcraft, is a living social force, a force that divides villages, sets friends, generations and even members of the same family against each other. In a small community it can cause social or even actual death. Frequently, however, it only reflects existing tensions and hostility and acts as a catalyst to bring these to a head. In so doing it relieves them; this enables the community to settle down peacefully, strong in the belief that another danger to itself and to its members has been removed.

CHAPTER III

THE *NG'AKA*

THE European, brought up to respect the difference between professional and quack, scientist and charlatan, is often prone to consider the witchdoctor and the leech or herbal doctor as practising two completely different professions. The latter he may believe to be misguided but approves his existence on the grounds that he resembles those European doctors of long ago who, whilst making many blunders, had honest intentions and faithfully strove to cure their patients of their maladies. For the former, however, he has nothing but harsh words and penalties, as may be seen from the following extract from the Laws : '4, Whoever shall be proved by habit or profession a witchdoctor or witchfinder shall be liable upon conviction to a fine . . . or to imprisonment. . . .'

This wide separation of the two professions has no counterpart in a central African environment. They are closely allied and, in many situations, no sharp distinction can be drawn between them. Both kinds of doctor are called *ng'aka*,[1] a strong indication of the proximity of their relationship in African eyes. This is not to say that the African does not recognize the differences between them. Any reasonably intelligent villager can explain that while the one deals directly with a malady using herbal and other medicines, the other, where witchcraft is diagnosed, cures the patient by parrying, by defeating and, if necessary, by killing the witch or sorcerer. The leech may give the patient a charm to wear or slip a needle under his skin, as a defence against magical attacks, but he is not thereby considered a witchdoctor. Because he recognizes that a particular illness is caused by a member of the spirit world, it does not mean that he considers that spirit a witch or a sorcerer. Perhaps one may obtain the best perspective if one considers the witchdoctor as a kind of specialist[2] dealing only with those troubles, not necessarily medical, caused by witches or by sorcerers. Just as the specialist is a superior

---

[1] *Nganga* among the Shona and other tribes south of the Zambezi. See Gelfand (1956) for a useful and comprehensive study of Shona *nganga*. These must not be confused with the Chokwe *nganga* who are *baloi*.

[2] Gelfand (1956.95) makes a similar distinction.

48

doctor, so the doctor of witchcraft, *ng'aka ya buloi*, is a superior *ng'aka*. He is indeed colloquially known as a 'big' doctor and is considered to be much more skilled and experienced than is his herbal counterpart.

The name, witchdoctor, implies that he is only concerned with witches, but this is not so. There is no suitable term to cover both anti-witchcraft and anti-sorcery; moreover, the term, witchdoctor, is too firmly established to be deposed. The term, doctor, is here used as a direct translation of *ng'aka* and includes both witchdoctor and leech. A witchdoctor is defined as one who acts either of his own volition, or at the request of another, against witches or sorcerers; aims to defeat their attacks; to make public their malevolent behaviour; to cure them of, or cause them to renounce their evil ways; and if necessary to kill and destroy them. A leech is concerned with those maladies not caused by witches or sorcerers, and his methods are to a certain extent similar to those employed by his European counterpart.

The ability to prepare charms or to heal the sick is not possessed solely by *ng'aka*. Just as in European society simple ailments, such as headaches or cuts and scratches, are treated without reference to a doctor, so also are many maladies treated without reference to an *ng'aka*. Some of the remedies are common knowledge; others are known only to a few. Similarly, a man requiring charms, for example, against snake-bite or to protect his cattle from crocodiles at a ford, goes to a layman who specializes in their manufacture. These specialists are not *ng'aka*.

The lay specialist is consulted only in simple matters, those where the cause of the malady appears obvious. Where the cause is not obvious or where the remedies or the charms of the lay specialist have no effect, thereby showing that there is some other hidden cause, the client must consult a diviner. He, in turn, will advise whether the services of an *ng'aka* are necessary.

The *ng'aka*, therefore, is employed where a malady or misfortune is caused by something mysterious and inexplicable to ordinary people. He is consulted only on the advice of a diviner though, as is explained later, he may himself be the diviner. Each lay specialist usually knows but a few remedies or charms. The *ng'aka*, however, unless he is a 'small' doctor able to treat only a limited number of ailments, as often are doctors of *muba* or of *sisongo*, is considered able to cure all those maladies that are treated by the lay specialist. His fees

Fig. 5. *Muba*

a and c. Figure (*Mwenda lutaka* or *Mwenda njangula*) in profile and face view
b. Genet skin with beads; placed on *muba* patient

are, of course, much higher, and it is understandable that, wherever possible, a man avails himself in the first instance of the services of the layman.

There is very little data available on the work of the lay specialist or on his role in Barotse village life. Attention is, therefore, restricted to the *ng'aka*, to the causes of the various maladies he treats, and to the methods and devices he employs to do so.

Belief in Magic

The anthropological arguments relating to the erroneous concepts of more primitive peoples on cause and effect have been too often expounded to bear repetition here. It is as well, however, for certain salient points to be borne in mind. The African, by reason of his traditional beliefs, attributes sickness and misfortune to a limited number of possible causes. By divination, he is able to find the apparent cause and then goes to the appropriate doctor or shrine. For him, magical or spiritual causes are of the same or of even greater importance than material ones. The European also has strong beliefs on the subject; the only difference being that he believes that for every misfortune there is a material or logical cause. For him, witchcraft ceased to exist as long ago as 1736, when the witchcraft laws ceased to deal with witches as such and concerned themselves purely with persons who *claimed* to possess magical powers. Such scepticism has had a profound effect on the more educated European's opinion of magic, and is reflected in his attitude to the beliefs and practices of the African peoples with whom he comes into contact.

Whether there is anything more in magic than mass hypnotism, sleight of hand, intuition, pure deceit or perhaps occasionally self-delusion on the part of the practitioners, is too wide a subject to be discussed here. Suffice it to say that, to the best of the writer's knowledge, no test has yet been made of magical claims under conditions satisfactory to both the practitioner and to the investigator.[1] The difficulties involved in making such a test are considerable: The magician never claims one hundred per cent success; the presence of the investigator may be considered to have an adverse effect on the rapport said to exist between the practitioner and the occult world; finally, should the test be successfully carried out and prove the magical powers of the claimant to be nil, the investigator must still have an uneasy feeling that perhaps the charlatan he has been working with is an exception and that there do exist, somewhere, genuine doctors and diviners. It is this belief, that failure discredits only the doctor and not the principle of magic itself, that keeps alive in the mind of the African his faith in the efficacy of magic. One success on the part of the doctor counts for more than any number of failures. Such could also be said of tests of magical practice. One positive re-

---

[1] This is a field which has been very inadequately covered. Most anthropologists start with the premise, 'magic is a spurious system of natural law as well as a fallacious guide of conduct; it is a false science as well as an abortive art' (Frazer, 1949.11), and merely concern themselves with the social and psychological effects resulting from its practice. For examples of researches based on the opposite premise, *vide* Seabrook (1929 and 1931) and Wright (1957). Such writers for the credulous public place too much emphasis on the bizarre and weird aspects of magico-religious practices.

sult, indicating that magical powers do exist, would have far greater importance than any number of negative results. Such a positive result is not likely to be achieved under scientific conditions and so an air of doubt and mystery must always cling to the subject of magic, until standards of education and health rise to the level where uncritical interest, and thereby belief in magic, wane.

Female Doctors

Ng'aka, like *baloi*, may be either male or female. Generally speaking, however, women tend to restrict themselves to herbal doctoring. Again a comparison may be drawn with the European medical field, where there are many female midwives[1] but comparatively few female surgeons. In Barotseland, the dangerous business of witchdoctoring is considered best left to the male sex.

Perhaps the belief that *baloi* are more frequently female may be connected with this tendency. A female witchdoctor, being herself a potential suspect, would have difficulty in gaining or holding the confidence of her clients. On the other hand, the female herbalist, specializing in the ailments of women or children, has a less detached feeling for the subject than has a male herbalist and has also the considerable advantage of being able to examine the patient herself. Where a male doctor treats a female patient, his wife usually carries out the physical examination. He must then diagnose and prescribe on the basis of her observations.

Selection and Training

The most common way by which a person comes to herbal doctoring is through sickness and successful treatment at the hands of a doctor. The latter, on completion of the treatment, often informs his patient that he may now himself practise this particular form of curing. Obviously the new *ng'aka*, if he intends to establish himself, has to make a success of his treatments, to gain at least local fame and to add further cures to his repertoire. All these three demands interact. The first development is usually that a neighbour or relative, knowing of his recent return to good health, brings to the new doctor a victim of the same sickness ; a cure produces the beginnings of his reputation. To keep this reputation and to enhance it, he must increase his store of knowledge. Should he lack interest or should he

---

[1] As was noted in Chapter II, the African midwife is especially liable to be accused of witchcraft.

make too many and too obvious blunders, he will slip back into the mediocrity whence he came.

Other ways of entering the field of herbal doctoring are those which are to be found in all crafts, inheritance and apprenticeship. Ambitious men have been known to travel considerable distances to the Congo or to Angola to study at the feet not only of herbal doctors but also of witchdoctors, diviners and witchfinders.

The witchdoctor, as befits a man who is a specialist, often rises from the ranks of the herbal doctors. Frequently, however, a layman may feel constrained to join this specialized branch of doctoring and so by-passes, and perhaps completely ignores his less spectacular, more humble colleagues, though when he falls ill of an ordinary complaint he has to place himself in their hands. One such case involved a herbal doctor who cured a witchdoctor of a *kaliloze* bullet wound in the leg. The gun used was of the modern variety.

Again, inheritance and apprenticeship play their part in filling the ranks of the witchdoctors. It is unlikely, however, that many recruits are found among those rescued from the attentions of *baloi*. They seem only too pleased to escape from their plight and shrink from further contact with sorcery.

The tendency to specialize, found among European scientists and medical men, has its counterpart among the Bantu. Just as the witchdoctor is a specialist among doctors, so is the *sikuyeti* doctor a specialist among witchdoctors. The difference would appear to be that whereas the ordinary witchdoctor is content, where possible, to remove the evil influence from his patient and to foil or expose the *muloi*, the *sikuyeti* doctor is much more ruthless; his aim is the destruction of the offending *muloi*. Some *baloi* are too powerful for the ordinary witchdoctor to tackle; the *sikuyeti* doctor, however, is able to trap and kill even the cleverest. The *kaliloze* doctor, it would appear is, for the LUNDA-LUVALE, what the *sikuyeti* doctor is for the LUYANA.[1]

It was to gatecrash this select group that there arrived on the scene in recent years a number of gunmen armed with the murderous new type of *kaliloze* gun. Whereas the traditional *kaliloze* gun is primarily employed against *baloi*, the new killers turned their weapons on anybody for a fee or for personal gain.[2] They are more aptly to be

---

[1] *Sikuyeti* and *kaliloze* are discussed later in this chapter.

[2] *Vide* such statements as: 'I used my gun also to bewitch a man who committed adultery with my wife.' 'It (the gun) was lent by a doctor to a client to threaten another . . . to obtain the beast about which there was a dispute.' 'This gun was used to kill a suspected adulteress.'

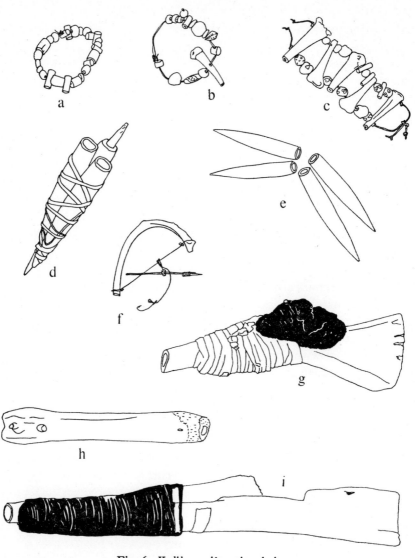

Fig. 6. *Kaliloze, sikuyeti* and *siposo*

a, b and c. *Ngoba siposo* bracelets
d and e. *Sikuyeti* sticks
f. *Kata*
g, h and i. Traditional *kaliloze* guns; bone barrels lashed (g and i) with bark strip to
   wooden stocks

named pseudo-*ng'aka* or, better still, *kaliloze* gunmen, and should not be confused with *kaliloze* doctors.

Herbal doctoring, witchdoctoring, *sikuyeti* doctoring, *kaliloze* doctoring ; one must not think of each of these as a watertight compartment into which a doctor enters and remains, never crossing into another compartment. Rather they are poles around which different types of doctor are grouped. There is nothing to prevent a doctor from changing his speciality ; neither is there anything to prevent his carrying on two, three or four at once. All depends on his personal preference, as does also the manner in which he combines them.

The reasons why a man becomes a witchdoctor are in many cases simple. Desire for prestige and a respected (or feared) position in society must be considerable. Perhaps, as Melland (1923.197) suggests, the intellectual demands of the profession serve as an outlet for an intelligence higher than the average ; 'he is very often a charming old village headman, with more intelligence than his peers by which one may often know him.' Desire for wealth and actual power, as opposed to prestige, is also a strong incentive. There are probably men who take up the profession from a sense of responsibility, a desire to shield their kin, their neighbours, the whole village from harm. On the other side, one finds the unpleasantly warped character who enters the lists ostensibly as a champion of his fellows but, in fact, in his own heart as their enemy. His hatred, resulting perhaps from some physical disability, could just as easily have led him into sorcery. The effect is the same, a reign of terror.

Whatever the motive and however the means by which the doctor is produced, his work demands a considerable amount of intelligence and, if not sincerity, then plausibility ; further, courage is required, for he is dabbling in matters that, according to belief, can easily cause not only his own death but also the maltreatment and destruction of his spirit.

Witchdoctors and Sorcerers

The witchdoctor makes use of the same magical forces[1] as does the sorcerer. In fact, the difference between them has often been stated as the difference between white and black magic. In many cases, the instruments with which the doctor handles these forces are the same

---

[1] *Mabibo* (LUYANA); *wanga* (LUNDA-LUVALE). White (1948b.83–84) considers *wanga* to be employed only by sorcerers. *Vide* McCulloch (1951.79 and 81) for a discussion of this point.

as those of the sorcerer. The analogy to be drawn is one of the spear, whose point and blade are dangerous either to malefactor or police-man, depending on who is wielding the weapon.

As may be expected some witchdoctors, there is no indication of just how many, combine their practice with that of sorcery. How pro-fitable such a combination proves is unknown. Because of the known oc-casional practising of such duplicity and because of the witchdoctor's potential misuse of his powers, most witchdoctors are feared by their neighbours. Of many it is rumoured that they practise sorcery and, in the sense of some of their practices being anti-social in nature, they sometimes do. Just as the sorcerer, to improve his knowledge of his craft, must undergo rites and perform duties which cause him to sink deeper into the pit of evil, so must the witchdoctor, striving to control similar magic powers for himself, carry out rites which in the ordinary course of events would label him a sorcerer.

In Chapter IV, the way in which the doctor depends for his clients, and in fact for his success, on the diviner is shown in detail. Here, it is only necessary to draw attention to this dependence and also to the fact that most herbal doctors find it useful to practise divining as well. Similarly, most witchdoctors practise witchfinding.

Guilds

It has been suggested that doctors form an organized body and Melland (1923.201) uses the word, guild, in discussing Kaonde witchdoctors. During the investigations there has been nothing to show that herbal doctors are so organized. The same applies to ordinary witchdoctors and also to *kaliloze* gunmen. They may be organized but there is no evidence to support the theory. More prob-ably the position is that, in a district or area, the doctors, both her-bal and witch, are known and are esteemed by the layman according to their experience, their success and their popularity. In a case which demands their intervention, the layman selects the doctor in whose powers he has the most confidence and whose charges he can afford to pay. A man seeking an apprenticeship acts on the same principles, attaching himself to the doctor he respects most and whose fees are not outside his pocket. When he graduates he will still, for many years, recognize the superior skill of his mentor and will ask his advice or even send difficult cases to him. Such practices re-sult in the grading of doctors in relation to each other and, of course, produce an illusion of organization or of a guild. The etiquette

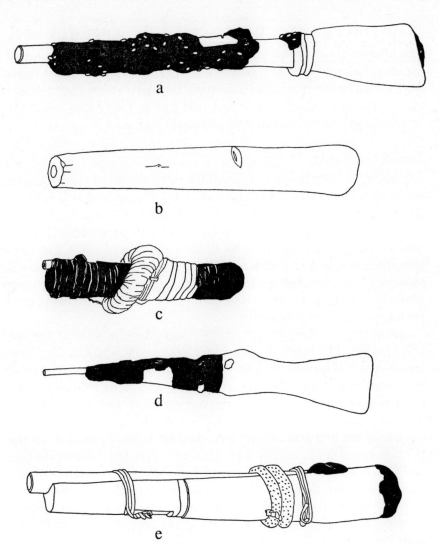

Fig. 7. *Kaliloze*

b. Wooden gun
c. Gun with cartridge case barrel
a, d and e. Guns with barrels of metal piping set on wooden stocks, partially covered
   with beeswax into which (a) lucky beans are impressed. Specimens a and e are known
   to have been used to commit murders (NRG, 1957 a, b and c)

whereby doctors respect each other does not help to dispel this
illusion.

In the case of the *sikuyeti* doctor, the picture is not a complete
blank. At Senanga, a man found in possession of *sikuyeti* sticks con-

fessed he was only a novice ; 'the chief *sikuyeti* doctor (one assumes of the area) had refused permission for him to be trained.' Such a statement could be interpreted as indicating the existence of an organized body led by one chief doctor. It could just as easily mean that the 'chief *sikuyeti* doctor' was merely *primus inter pares*.

Doctors and Society

Finally, it is of interest to consider the position of the *ng'aka* in ordinary society. Obviously the successful doctor, and it is only he that really interests us, is held in awe and even fear by his neighbours. Since he charges for his services he is likely to be wealthy. By this wealth and by his reputation, he holds a position of some considerable influence and importance. Whether, however, this position is translated into something concrete, such as a headmanship, is rather unlikely, to judge by the small proportion of headmen who have been found to be witchdoctors.

According to British law, there is no place in society for the witchdoctor. The result is that, where evidence is forthcoming, he is arrested and imprisoned. The African considers this to be unkind treatment of his defenders, protects them and often refuses to bear witness against them. Admittedly, during 1956 and 1957, this behaviour seems to have been reversed but, on closer investigation, one finds that the first accusations were against *kaliloze* gunmen. In the general hysteria old scores were paid off; first the *kaliloze* doctors and finally all doctors, sorcerers, diviners and so on were included and accusations flew thick and fast. Even so, the complaint was sometimes heard that the Government was arresting the wrong people, the witchdoctors, and allowing the true troublemakers, the *baloi*, to escape.

Since their relatively recent arrival in the territory, the prestige of European doctors, both Government and missionary, has steadily increased at the expense of their African counterparts. Symon (1950. 1–2) observed at Mankoya :

the number of native doctors has been considerably reduced because of a growing faith in the efficacy of European medicines. This is particularly noticeable in areas adjacent to the Boma dispensary where the work of the native doctor has almost died out. . . . I have been told, and I have no reason to disbelieve it, that until 20 years ago it was unheard of for a native doctor to travel around the District, and neighbouring Districts, soliciting custom—it is certainly now the accepted practice to do this and those living near the Boma travel as far afield as Solwezi, Mumbwa, Namwala, and some even to the Copperbelt.

That African doctors still have a strong hold and in many cases thriving practices is well known ; the extent of these practices was forcibly demonstrated in Barotseland when, as a result of the investigations, many doctors were imprisoned and many others, for fear of a similar fate, stopped practising. The effect was soon felt at the hospitals and dispensaries, where there was a sharp rise in the numbers of sick coming for treatment.

In recent years, perhaps because of the competition he affords, the *ng'aka* has borrowed from and copied the European doctor in a number of ways, though as often as not it would appear that the essential elements of a practice or process are ignored. On the homoeopathic principle that the effect the medicine has on the patient is the same that it has on the malady, treatment by injection has been eagerly accepted in central Africa, both by urban and by rural patients. This may have given the *ng'aka* the idea of inserting needle charms. Whatever its origin, the needle charm now enjoys a popularity comparable to that of the injection needle. Whether the premedication of the needle is derived from the sterilization process of surgical equipment is also an interesting possibility. A similar imitation of European medical practice was carried on by a Luvale doctor. After treating the patient and administering medicines, he took blood from her finger tips for examination, in order to determine what effect his medicines had had.

One of the features of local beliefs, noted during the interrogation both of witnesses and of accused, was that certain doctors, both herbal and witch, claimed to have been licensed by the Government and to be carrying on their practices with its full approval. This arose in two different ways. Firstly, some chiefs and *indunas* have, on occasions, provided herbal doctors with letters stating that their practices were not illegal. One may assume that, at the time such a letter was issued, an examination was made by the chief or *induna* of the practices. No consideration could, however, have been given to the possibility that the herbal doctor might not restrict himself to those practices. These letters are of no legal value, for no authority has the right to issue permits. Even so, they are accepted by gullible clients.

Secondly, a number of doctors, and also diviners and witchfinders,

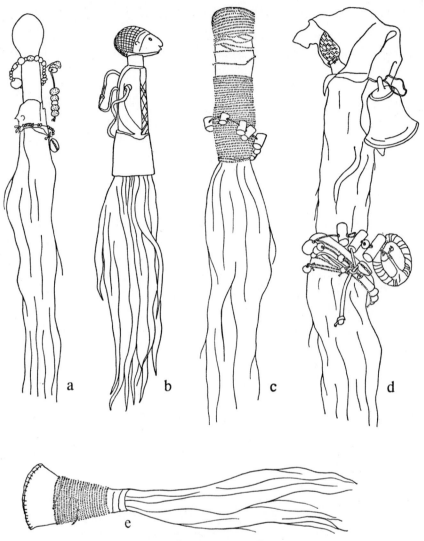

Fig. 8. Flyswitches (i)

a. Switch with wooden handle; Venetian (and other) beads
b. Lozi raindoctor's flyswitch; carved wooden handle
c. Heavily beaded switch
d. Switch with basketry handle, bell, beads, etc.
e. Switch with beaded gourd handle

find it politic to arm themselves with a piece of paper, preferably one which bears some indication that it originates from a hospital. If the paper also bears the signature or name stamp of the medical officer-in-charge, so much the better. This practice has been developed, and

A flooded homestead on the Barotse plain; preparing to move as the waters rise

Four LUNDA-LUVALE women accused of necrophagy; Kalabo, 1957

one finds cases of audacious doctors who 'send up' difficult cases to the local medical officer whose name graces their 'licence'. One witchdoctor-cum-witchfinder even went so far as to sign a letter, in which he stated the names of the guilty *baloi*, with a combination of his own name and that of the local European doctor. Like many of his colleagues, this witchdoctor, who already had two convictions under the Witchcraft Ordinance, stoutly maintained even after sentence that he was licensed to practice.

Licences have no legal value and witchdoctors are not sheltered by the authorities. However, since working in Barotseland the writer has been reliably informed that, in a district in another part of the territory, there lives an African doctor,

who enjoys a considerable local reputation for searching out witchdoctors, sorcerers and those who have cast spells against others.

His services have frequently been requested by Chiefs for their areas and he has been allowed to make investigations provided he reports fully the work he has done. I might add that it is said that his methods of divining are very different to those normally employed in the District and this undoubtedly contributes to the reputation he has built up.

An excellent example of the exception that proves the rule.

At the present time, the position of the Barotse *ng'aka*, whatever his specialization, is a difficult one. He still fills a very real need, yet must practise in secret for fear of arrest. His clientele too, becoming more worldly-wise, requires more than the stock treatments to deal with their problems. As will be seen in the remainder of this chapter, the causes of their maladies are changing as a result of contact with other tribes and with the modern world. To keep pace, the *ng'aka* must also modernize his techniques and equipment.

CAUSES OF MISFORTUNE

Sickness and misfortune are believed, especially by the victim and his kin, to be caused by *baloi* or by spirits. These spirits may be ancestral but there are also others which are capable of causing harm. Of course, as in any society, bystanders not directly involved are quite willing to accept that such troubles have resulted from natural causes. Careless handling of an axe must certainly result in a wound ; failure to moor a canoe securely, at a time when the floods are rising, will most probably result in the disappearance of the canoe. The victim, however, all too frequently blames the wound or the loss on *baloi* or on other non-human agencies.

For convenience, the work of the leech and of the witchdoctor are described separately below. By the nature of the investigation, the information available for the latter is far more plentiful than it is for the former. All too many of the ailments mentioned in the case records are mere names with little or no accompanying data. Fortunately, a valuable record was made a few years ago of the preparations and uses of the native medicines used by the doctors of Mankoya district (Symon, 1950), and, more recently, there has been published a similar work on Balovale and other districts (Gilges, 1955). The following notes should be read in conjunction with these two reports.

ANCESTRAL SPIRITS

Ancestors intervene for a variety of reasons in the lives of their descendants. In some cases, an illness is believed to have been caused by any one of a number of offended ancestors ; in others, it is ascribed to one in particular. The cures for such troubles usually require the propitiation of the ancestor concerned rather than treatment of the patient himself though, where the malady is physical rather than psychical, a combination of the two may be employed.

While an offended ancestor may merely afflict his descendant with misfortune, medical or otherwise, he often prefers to enter and inhabit his body. Exorcism, followed by propitiation, is then necessary before the descendant can return to his normal state. Such actions on the part of the ancestor may be ascribed to a variety of causes. He may be offended by the misbehaviour, moral or otherwise, of his kin ; he may feel he is being neglected, that a proper respect has not been shown him, or that they have failed to make offerings on appropriate occasions. Propitiation and improved behaviour should cause him to cease his attacks. Should a man pass, by misfortune, through an invisible village of ancestral spirits he will fall ill, and again propitiation and atonement are necessary to soothe the offended spirits. When an ancestor wishes to draw attention to himself, either to ensure the perpetuation of his name by a child or to indicate his selection of a particular descendant to inherit the craft (hunting, blacksmithing, doctoring) which he himself once practised on earth, he enters the body of that unfortunate, thus making him ill. A diviner duly discovers the reason and the cure is obvious.

Mahamba

Possession by ancestral spirits (*lihamba*, pl. *mahamba*) occupies an important place among the magico/medical beliefs of the LUNDA-LUVALE. The verb root, *hamba*, may be translated as 'resurrect'. McCulloch (1951.76)[1] observes that the *mukishi* and the *lihamba* are

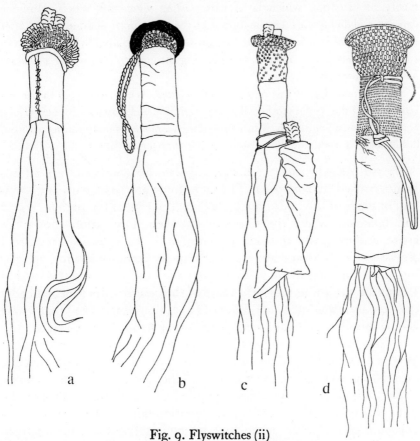

Fig. 9. Flyswitches (ii)

Various switches each with a basketry handle

distinctly separate; 'the *mukishi* is the abstract conception of an ancestral spirit, while the *lihamba* is its overt manifestation.'

McCulloch (1951.77–78) describes the various kinds of traditional spirits or *mahamba vausoko* ('kinship' *mahamba*; so called because the ancestral spirit was originally thought to emerge only within the matrilineal kin group)—*mahamba valusemo*, affecting

[1] Following White (1949).

female fertility ; *mahamba vaungyanga,* which are the spirits of hunters and which usually only affect males ; and others such as spirits of diviners or masked dancers.

The old *mahamba* survive, but are rarely heard of today. A new series has emerged, largely divorced from the ancestral cult, and has become an important theory of causation which is in part ousting witchcraft beliefs. Hunters, dancers, and diviners are less important to the community and less feared after their death. The new *mahamba* are usually said to be acquired by infection from a person possessed by a *lihamba*, or by passing through an area where a *lihamba* has been exorcized . . . .

The introduction of this new type of *mahamba* is clearly related to the enlargement of the spatial world following migration and contact with new tribes, and finally with Europeans. The cause of the *mahamba* is now transferred from dead ancestors within the kin group to living strangers outside it.

Siyaya (liyaya), sisongo (cisongo, kayongo) and *tundundu* are all ailments caused by *mahamba*. The symptoms are headaches and swelling of parts of the body ; *sisongo* affects the legs of the patient, *siyaya* and *tundundu* affect the chest or stomach. Divination shows the cause, and exorcism and skilled treatment by an *ng'aka* are required. These *mahamba* would appear to be true ancestral spirits for, according to informants, *siyaya* is known to have existed among the Lozi of Lewanika's reign in the early years of the century. Its acceptance by the LUYANA was such that Kuntz (1932.131) considered that it was a Lozi ailment. In Mankoya, on the other hand, Symon (1950, 72–73, 76–77) noted that *liyaya* appeared only to affect the immigrant Wiko (LUNDA-LUVALE) peoples of the district. He records that the exorcism is assisted, in cases of *sisongo* and *liyaya*, by medicine taken orally and by hot fomentations applied to the affected parts of the body. He does not, as does Kuntz, mention inhalations. Modern *mahamba*, such as, '*ndeke* (aeroplane), which is derived by infection from areas where planes are frequently seen. This *lihamba* is said to cause weakness of the legs when walking' (McCulloch, 1951.78), were also encountered during the investigation, and one of these, *bindele*, is fully discussed in Chapter VI.

BUSH SPIRITS

Some complaints are associated with bush spirits rather than with ancestral spirits, though informants point out that nowadays distinctions between the two groups are less and less frequently drawn.

Muba

This is a very common complaint which takes the form of madness or fits. While it is believed to be a relative newcomer to Barotseland, many doctors specialize in it and would appear to be well-patronized, although the ailment and its treatment were only noted in Sesheke and Senanga case records, where more attention was paid to herbal doctoring. The doctors concerned were mainly LUYANA and ASSIMI-LATED LUYANA, though Gluckman's (1951.85) Lozi informants believed *muba* to be of Totela origin.

Treatment is by exorcism of the spirit and is surprisingly uniform, involving in almost all cases the use of a genet skin as described below. This uniformity is probably due to there having been insufficient time as yet for alternative remedies to have become fashionable, and to the fact that so many *muba* patients become *muba* doctors, employing the method they know from experience to be successful. One informant even suggests that this adoption of the profession is almost involuntary. It is to be remarked also that *muba* doctors rarely treat other forms of illness.

The spirits, *mwenda-njangula* and *mwenda-lutaka*, which are considered responsible for *muba* attacks, are believed to be creatures in human form, the limbs of one side of which are alive and, of the other side, of reeds covered with beeswax. The spirits live in dense bush and cannot come out into the light for fear of the wax melting. Gluckman (1951.85) notes that they are : '(Lozi) demons of the bush and the Plain respectively, which have half-human bodies and are fiery red. They are of both sexes. Should one of these spirits desire a man or woman, it will try to kidnap him or her, and can at least strike with severe illness.' If a human has the misfortune to meet one of these spirits there is a struggle. Should the human win, he is taught how to cure *muba*; should he be defeated, the spirit enters his body, he sickens and dies. This is an interesting rationalization of the struggles of a madman. Should he be cured, he has obviously defeated his tormentor and, in so doing, has learned how to help others suffering from the same affliction.

Half-figures, representing *mwenda-lutaka* or *mwenda-njangula*, are occasionally carved (Fig. 5(a) and (b)). One doctor used his to divine the ailment by rubbing it on the ground. The principle was that of friction, as is described in Chapter IV. This doctor also claimed, after his trial, that he dipped the figure into a pot of medicine and rubbed the flat surface over the patient's body as part of the treatment.

In another case, while the patient is inhaling steam from a pot of medicines, a stick, some two feet in length and decorated with a necklet of beads, is stuck into the ground beside him. If the patient is suffering from *muba,* he will so indicate by beginning to dance.

Treatment for *muba* usually involves the use of a genet (*sipa*) skin to one end of which is fastened a string or two of beads (Fig. 5(c)). A typical treatment is for the patient to be covered with a blanket, beneath which is also placed a pot of hot steaming medicines. The patient inhales the fumes and, meanwhile, the genet skin is placed on his head. The doctor dances to help drive out the spirit, and the patient usually joins him. According to informants, the operative factor is the genet skin which, being applied on two days, will effect a cure on the third.

PHYSICAL CAUSES

The majority of minor ailments are considered to present medical rather than magical problems and are treated accordingly. Such problems range from trachoma of the eye to gonorrhea, headaches to snakebite. The ailment may be ascribed to some fanciful cause, and cause and symptoms may not be distinguished from each other. The following are a few examples.

NDUME	CAUSE	the presence of a snake (python) in the stomach. (This is not a spirit.)
	SYMPTOMS	stomach pains and a miscarriage in early pregnancy.
MBOMA	CAUSE	as above.
	SYMPTOMS	stomach pains and miscarriage, or perhaps even still-birth.
NAMWEMBA	CAUSE	infection. The patient is considered to have eaten the remains of food (e.g. porridge) left or given by somebody suffering from *namwemba.*
	SYMPTOMS	intermittent stomach pains and a swelling on the left side of the stomach or intestines.

66

CILUMBA   CAUSE natural.

SYMPTOMS swollen testicles which may even burst the scrotum. This ailment does not seem to have any effect on a man's sexual or procreative powers.

SNAKE-BITE   CAUSE natural.

SYMPTOMS severe pain, etc.

TREATMENT the wound is cut open and a tourniquet applied. The patient is given human faeces in water to drink. This provokes vomiting.

As may be expected, anatomical and physiological knowledge is poor, and surgery is rarely practised. Sprains are poulticed and simple dislocations corrected, though these may be done by laymen and not necessarily by doctors. Flesh wounds are bandaged and perhaps medicated; foreign bodies, either actual or supposed, may be extracted by sucking or cupping. Pimples and boils may be poulticed and, if need be, lanced.

Medicine, either in solution or in powder form, is usually administered orally though, on occasions, the rectum[1] or vagina may be used. Abortifacients, such as powdered *mutata* (*Securidaca longipedunculata*) roots, are inserted into the vagina. Such practices are highly dangerous and death often results. This is also a common method of suicide (Gilges, 1955.7; Fanshawe and Hough, 1960.11–12). In cases of diarrhoea the medicine may not be inserted directly into the body, but may rather be rubbed into the surface of a wooden stool on which the patient is required to seat himself.

Emetics and purgatives, administered orally, are also commonly employed. The effect an ailment has on a local area of the body, irrespective of whether it is actually located in that part, influences the treatment. Thus while, for headaches, the temples and the back of the neck may be the object of attention, in cases of fever attention may be given to the back or limbs, according to where the patient feels pain or heat. The treatment usually consists of rubbing medicine, usually a paste or ointment made up of pounded and often

---

[1] Sigerist (1951) gives an interesting illustration of a Kwanyama (S. Angola) woman administering an enema to her child by blowing the liquid, through a reed, directly into the rectum (ibid. Figs. 51 and 52). The Barotse use the same technique; the enema may consist of *mulia* (*Diplorrhyncus mossambicensis*) roots in solution.

charred roots bonded with oil or fat, into a number of shallow cuts made in the skin of the affected limb or part.

Blood-letting is a common practice and is usually done with a horn (*mulumeho*) or similarly shaped gourd (Fig. 20(e)). The mouth of the horn is placed over the incision and a vacuum created by the

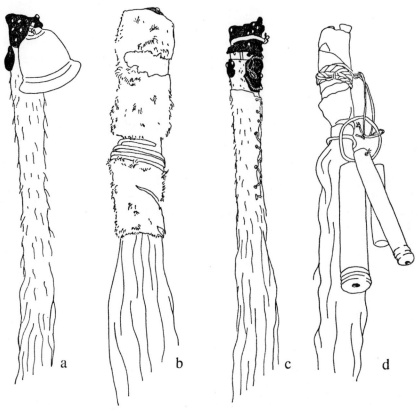

a   b   c   d

Fig. 10. Flyswitches (iii)

a–c. Various switches, each with skin-wrapped handles, and beeswax with lucky beans
    at the butt
d. Switch with cloth-wrapped handle

doctor sucking through the peak. To seal the vacuum, he closes the small hole in the peak with beeswax, using his tongue and teeth. The outside of the peak is liberally smeared with beeswax to facilitate this. To break the vacuum, the seal is pierced with a grass stalk and the congealed blood contained in the horn poured off into a dish. Two or three horns may be employed, either in succession or at the same time, and the amount of blood-letting depends on the doctor's decision and perhaps the client's patience. Cupping horns are also employed without reference to an *ng'aka* or even to a lay specialist, in much the same way as aspirins are employed in an European household.

Inhalations of steam from boiling roots are commonly prescribed, not only in true medical cases but also in cases of spirit possession as discussed earlier. For eye and ear troubles, small quantities of medicines in solution are usually administered to the affected organ. Like most primitive peoples, the Bantu possess no standard measurements of space, time, volume or weight. It is not surprising, therefore, that the dosage prescribed by the *ng'aka* varies considerably from doctor to doctor and from case to case.

Finally, it must be remembered, when considering the whole subject of native doctoring, that the principle upon which treatment is based is 'payment by results' and the decision as to whether or when the treatment proves successful is left to the patient or, more often, to his relatives. Except in very serious cases, a doctor/diviner charges but a small sum for divining or diagnosing the malady and only receives his real payment after a cure has been effected. Common charges are 3d or 6d for diagnosis and 10s for a cure.

Baloi

The attacks of *baloi* are intended to cause death or considerable material misfortune and have already been discussed in Chapter II. The methods by which the attacks of *baloi* are combated are described in the next section.

WEAPONS AND METHODS
PROTECTIVE MAGIC

Charms (Fig. 19) of this type are among the most popular, and are certainly the most frequently used means of defeating witchcraft attacks. They may be used to protect property or persons, according to the situation, and may be of a specific or general nature to ward off current attacks or merely possible future attacks. A few examples are as follows :

A medicinal root strung on a necklace and worn by a pregnant woman or a babe against attacks by *baloi* desiring a foetus or small child. This is a very common charm.

A horn, containing burnt medicine, to prevent spirits from entering the house (Figs. 11 and 12). Such a horn may be placed in the ground, near the head of a sick person, to prevent bewitchment. Tortoise-shell containers may also be used for this purpose (Fig. 13(h), (i) and (j)). Similarly, a medicated gourd (*ndombwe*) may be set in the doorway and a live coal placed in the top in order to keep trouble away from the sleeping inhabitant. More sinister methods are the replacement of the gourd and coal with the teeth of a puff-adder, set in a medicated horn; a marauding spirit would be bitten. Similarly, a patient may be given a skull (Fig. 13) or other part of a human corpse as a protective charm. Such are considered powerful charms. Although the spirit is not sent by a sorcerer, it is convenient to note here that a Luvale widower may be given a charm to protect him from the spirit of his dead wife.

Mention must also be made of the use of needles for protection. Just as in an ordinary case of illness, so in a case of witchcraft the doctor is nowadays prone to slip a needle into his patient to protect him in the future. More is said on this subject below.

There is one form of protection which is a form of taboo. For example, after establishing by divination that witchcraft has been the cause of death, a doctor may place a charm upon the corpse so that any person or animal who tries to eat it will die. In the same way a Luvale husband, suspicious of his wife's loyalty, may place a charm beneath her pillow. Should she then commit adultery, her lover's testicles will swell and she herself may die.

Finally, the following Lozi account of how protection from the attacks of *baloi* may be obtained for one's spirit, will be of interest:

A man, now 68, took hair, blood and nail clippings from his young granddaughter and had a doctor make them up into a medicine and place this inside an egg. The man then took the egg to the graveyard for a night and slept there. Later he threw it in a pool. Thus he changed spirits with the girl and thereby hid his own spirit from witchcraft attacks. Therefore, he will live for a long time. The girl (now 33 years) suspected first when her first child died then when their (i.e. her and her grandfather's) illnesses coincided. She complained for fear of dying young.

PUNITIVE PROTECTION

To commission a witchdoctor to provide this service is a much more serious matter than merely to purchase a defensive charm, and is always restricted to specific witchcraft attacks. The client, and even more so the doctor, are entering into the magical field proper. In a sense, the doctor now sets out to be both sword and buckler for his client, and by this action attracts to himself the attention of the *muloi* concerned. Unless either the sorcerer swiftly succeeds in killing his victim, or one of the combatants withdraws from the field, there ensues a battle royal of repeated thrust and parry. The hazards

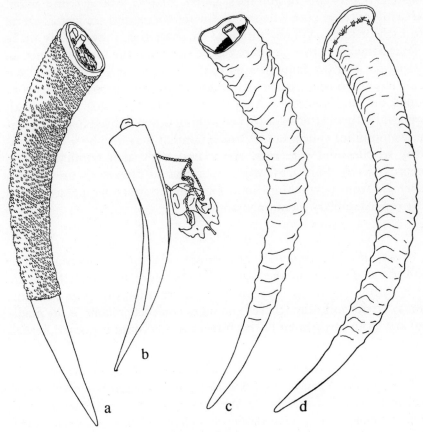

Fig. 11. Horns (i)

Various medicine horns; specimen a is covered with a sisal sleeve resembling crochet work

of the battle are increased by the fact that most of the invisible weapons which fly through the ether are of a boomerang nature; should they be parried, they recoil on their sender, who must then parry both them and those of his opponent. If both opponents are determined then there can be but one end, the death of one or both, or perhaps of all three. The criterion is who has the greater skill and experience, the sorcerer or the witchdoctor or, more prosaically, the ability of the client to pay the fees of the latter.[1]

FAMILIARS (Figs. 2, 3 and 4)

In Chapter II, the use of familiars by sorcerers has already been discussed. Most types of familiars, *likishi*, *nameya*, *kanenga*, and so on, are employed by both sorcerer and witchdoctor and are just as useful to each of them. When employed by the latter, they usually make direct attacks on the agents or on the person of the former. Thus, an Mbunda *kanenga* familiar was reputed to be able to remove evil spirits molesting a patient. Another Kwangwa *kanenga* was used to smell out and destroy *baloi*, the owner boasting that every death caused by these attacks or by bewitching others, raised his own prestige among his colleagues. A *likishi* familiar may also be used to destroy witches and sorcerers. Associated with such familiars is the mask (*likishi*) (Fig. 3(b)) worn by a Shanjo diviner to prevent his enemies from bewitching him. The same powers are possessed by the other familiars mentioned above.

SIPOSO

Very little has come to light during the investigations concerning the effect *siposo* has on its victim. It is, therefore, extremely fortunate that Symon (1950.74–75) gathered information on *siposo* in Mankoya district and, since there is no more complete record of the medical aspect and treatment of the ailment, his account is quoted here in full :

Siposo—A deadly charm or medicine believed to be effective from afar.

SYMPTOMS—A patient will feel a sharp pain in any part of the body which may be accompanied by sickness. After treatment for other diseases that have similar symptoms being unsuccessful the patient will go to a divining doctor (*mulauli*) who will divine to see if the patient is suffering from *siposo*. After this divination the patient will go to a native doctor for treatment.

TREATMENT—(*a*) A *mulumeho* (a horn made from the outside of the horn of a cow or an ox) is used to draw out the pain. A mixture is prepared from the roots of the *Mafula* (*Combretum sp.*) which are soaked in cold water for a few minutes. Small cuts, about half an inch in length are made around the region of the pain. The *mulumeho* is then applied to the first of these cuts, after having

---

[1] 'The richer of the two continues to make black magic while the poorer man unable to continue paying the witchdoctor's fees succumbs from superstitious fear, pines and dies.' (Singleton-Fisher, 1949.22.)

been soaked in the mixture prepared as above. The *mulumeho* has a small hole at the pointed end and the doctor, after placing the wide end of the horn over the cut, withdraws the air from inside and blocks this hole so that the vacuum so formed sucks blood from the cut. The *mulumeho* is left in position for about five

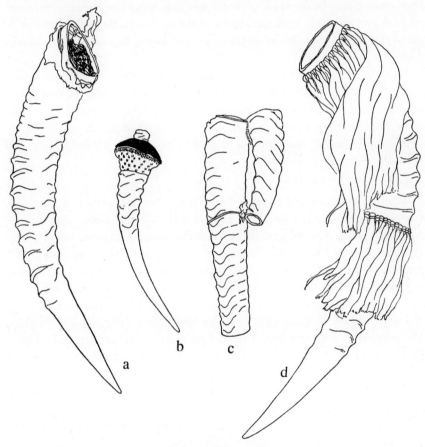

Fig. 12. Horns (ii)
Various medicine horns

minutes by which time an estimated tablespoon of blood has been withdrawn. The blood is then put into a calabash and stirred with a stick to see whether any foreign body has also been withdrawn from the body. If nothing is found then the same procedure is adopted with the second cut. If this is not successful a hot fomentation is applied to the area of the pain, the fomentation is prepared by boiling the mixture of the *Mafula* tree already prepared. The patient is then left for the night with this fomentation applied.

(*b*) The procedure with the *mulumeho* is again repeated on the second day in the event of the first day's treatment having not proved successful. If this second treatment with the *mulumeho* does not effect a cure then hot fomentations are again applied and the patient left until the third day when the same treatment is once again given. In the event of no foreign body being discovered or improvement shown after this third application of the *mulumeho*, the patient cannot be cured and remains to suffer in silence or to move to the dispensary for treatment there.

NOTE. The specialist who treats *siposo* alleges that this treatment is very successful and he usually finds something in the blood—sometimes a bead or a piece of stone. It is always something tangible and not the figment of his imagination. No charms or drums are used in the treatment of this disease, but quite often a rattle (*mulai*) made from a calabash with some beads inside, is played when the *mulumeho* is in position.

FEES CHARGED 15s.

It is only necessary to add a few notes to this very full account. Firstly needles, nails or flies, presumably all invisible, may act as *siposo* carrying agents and, it may further be presumed, will be discovered in the blood. Lightning or aeroplanes may also be agents. Secondly, at least in the rest of Barotseland, *siposo* has a very strong connection with needle charms, both in defensive and offensive magic, and also with *kaliloze* guns. Thirdly, projection may be via medicine-filled python-skin belts or armbands (Fig. 18). Fourthly, the importance of the *ngoba* bead bracelets must be stressed. These bracelets (Fig. 6(a), (b) and (c)) are worn to ward off or enable the wearer to project *siposo* and are only to be found in the possession of real sorcerers or *ng'aka*, who obtain them from those *siposo* doctors who are able to control *siposo* as well as to cure its effects. Each bracelet consists of pieces of medicated roots, beads and cowrie shells, the last-named symbolizing eyes which prevent people looking directly into the eyes of the wearer and, it may be assumed, thereby bewitching him. The beads are often Venetian beads (i.e. spotted), probably for the same reason.

The only information available on the monetary value of *siposo* is that one informant from Mongu paid £5 for needles and the power to project *siposo*; another from Kalabo paid one cow for a needle to give the strength necessary for killing witches (*baloi*) with what he called a '*siposo* gun' (*kaliloze*).

74

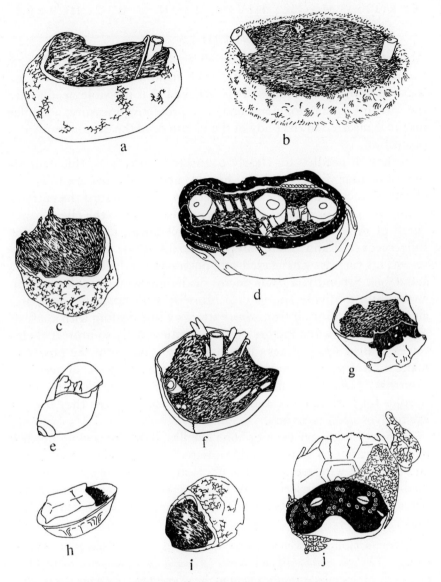

Fig. 13. Medicine containers (i); skulls and shells

a–d, f and g. Portions of human skulls
e. Shell of an *Acontias* snail
h–j. Tortoise shells

Specimens a, c, i and j are covered with closely fitting sisal caps resembling crochet work. Specimen b has a cap of skin; specimen d, a cap of coarse cloth. Beeswax and lucky beans have been added to specimens d, g and j.

NEEDLES

According to Lawrance,[1] needle charms were first heard of in or about 1928 from people coming back from Wankie, and were associated with *siposo* killings. It is believed that invisible needles are the carrying agents for *siposo* and, as a protective measure, a similar needle is inserted in the body of the victim or of the person requiring protection.

Although needles are clearly connected with *siposo*, this connection is of four different kinds. Firstly, needle charms are found in clients of doctors or diviners as protection, either against the entry of the *siposo* agent or against its re-entry subsequent to the client being cured of *siposo* disease. Since, in many instances, the patient is not fully recovered and often barely conscious when the needle is inserted, his surprise when taxed with possession of the charm is understandable. Secondly, a *siposo* doctor or diviner wears needles both to enable him to divine and to deal properly with *siposo* sickness, and also to protect himself from *siposo* attacks while dealing with a case of *siposo*. Thirdly, witchdoctors possess needles partly to protect themselves against *siposo* attacks but more so to give them the power to make such attacks on sorcerers. The latter also make use of needles.[2] Fourthly, *kaliloze* gunmen, and also some *kaliloze* doctors, wear needles for both defence and offence because the guns they use are themselves *siposo* weapons.

Although ordinary gramophone needles, halves of sewing needles and, according to some unsubstantiated claims, nails, small horns and pieces of wire are used, it is necessary for the charm to be duly medicated before insertion. A Luchazi herbal doctor, who numbered among his patients a *kaliloze* gunman, claimed to use the following recipe:

Prepare a medicine, which among other things contains pieces of *situndu-bwanga* (?*Xylopia antunessii*) and *ilutwa* (*Ximenia americana*) tree roots. Place the needle in this mixture and set light to the whole. Charcoal from the result is rubbed on the patient's chest and the hot needle is pushed into the body.

In most cases, the insertion is made on the chest, either in the centre or, more commonly, in the thicker flesh above either breast. Occasionally the needle may be placed elsewhere, over the shoulder

[1] Senanga district files, 1957.

[2] Strangely enough, no needle charms were recorded as being in the possession of the various suspected necrophagers arrested.

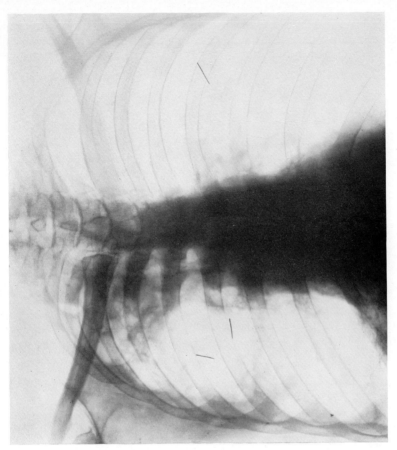

X-ray plate showing three needles *in situ*

A patient is prepared for an herbal inhalation

blade or in the arm, but such variations are rare. The wearers of needles are usually male, perhaps because men are considered to be more likely to suffer from *siposo* troubles or possibly to be more frequently concerned with dangerous magic.

Usually, a needle wearer has but the one needle charm, though on occasions the possession of two or even three needles in the body has been recorded. The only satisfactory explanation is that such a person is considered, by reason of his condition or activities, to stand in an unusually dangerous position with regard to *siposo*; this demands for him or her, special protection. Thus, a *kaliloze* doctor or a tubercular patient may each turn to the charm as a means of protection.

More sinister interpretations have been placed upon the presence of a needle charm. One known *kaliloze* gunman in Kalabo, himself wearing more than one needle, repeatedly and fiercely asserted that the possession of two or more needles is a sign that the owner has killed a man by *siposo*. Other informants agree with this interpretation. Another Kalabo accused stated that, with the first needle and a borrowed *kaliloze* gun, a gunman must kill somebody before completing his initiation and receiving a second needle and his own personal gun. In Mongu too it was asserted, this time in a letter to the boma, 'when a man has put in a needle without having killed a person the needle will come out by itself but if you have killed a person the needle will stay in your chest.'

The popularity of the needle charm is undoubted.[1] Over 190 cases were reported during the investigations before the local people, realizing that the possession of needle charms was an offence, extracted them. The scars are small and very soon heal.

Medical officers have pointed out that they have long known of the existence of this modern form of charm but have never attached much importance to it. Although no systematic widespread survey of the distribution of the needle charm has been made, it is known to occur both within the territory—Barotseland, the contiguous Southern and North-Western Provinces, especially Balovale and Livingstone districts, the Copperbelt and Eastern Province—and outside in Wankie, Nyasaland, Angola and even Kenya.

The primary origins of this type of charm are obscure. There may

---

[1] A sample of X-ray records taken in the African Hospital, Livingstone, produced over 5 per cent of plates showing needles. Since this sample was made irrespective of age or sex it may be assumed that the percentage of adult male plates was higher than this.

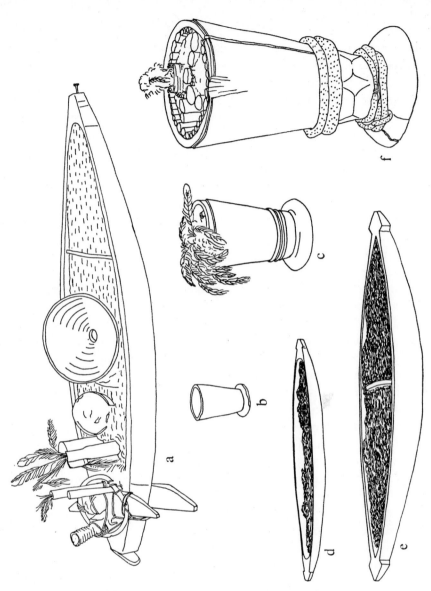

Fig. 14. Medicine containers (ii); wooden

a. A *fulai* (i.e. 'fly' = aeroplane) charm   d and e. Miniature canoes

b, c and f. Miniature mortars

possibly be some traditional practice from which it has sprung, such as the insertion of a medicated thorn; indeed the practice of discovering foreign bodies inserted into the flesh or bloodstream is very old and very widespread. The immediate cause of its recent development must be, however, the example of the European medical practice of injection. As has already been stated the popularity and, at the same time, the respect that this form of treatment has achieved among Africans is considerable, and the desire of an *ng'aka* to emulate his European colleague must be very strong. The belief that an invisible needle is the carrying agent for *siposo* was probably a fortuitous factor, inspired by some sufferer's belief or delusion that his sufferings began with a pin-prick. Certainly, as Symon mentions in his account of *siposo* disease, the symptoms are that 'a patient will feel a sharp pain . . .'. There may perhaps be some connection too with the method of attack, described in Chapter II, where the *muloi* sticks an actual needle into her victim.

Needles of considerable age, in one instance approximately thirty years, have been extracted; such needles often partially disintegrate in the body. On the other hand, according to the records available, mainly admissions by wearers, the majority of the needles have been inserted since 1950. This phenomenon is discussed in Chapter VII.

KALILOZE GUNS (Figs. 6 and 7)

The difference between the *kaliloze* doctor and the *kaliloze* gunman has already been explained. Both, however, appear to hold the same beliefs concerning their weapons and practise the same protective and preparative rituals.

The name, *kaliloze*, is derived from the Luvale verb, *kuloza*, 'to kill' or 'to bewitch'. Another name, nowadays only rarely used, is *wuta wa mufuko* which may be freely translated as 'a gun made from an armbone'. The literal meaning of *wuta* is 'a bow'.

The traditional form of gun is a human limb-bone from which one of the epiphyses has been removed. The exposed stem is hollowed out and the remaining epiphysis acts as a butt. Just in front of this butt is bored a touch-hole. Sometimes the bone is mounted on a wooden stock, or the whole gun may be carved from a solid piece of wood. The material for such a stock, and presumably in the latter case for the whole gun, is taken from the poles of a stretcher which has been used to carry a corpse to its grave. Where barrel and stock are separate they are lashed together, usually with bark strip. White (1948.100) states that the leg-bone of a marabou stork is sometimes used and that he observed a specimen in Mwinilunga. All other authorities only mention the use of human bones.

The modern type of *kaliloze* has as its main feature a metal barrel, often a piece of gas or similar piping or, occasionally, a heavy rifle bullet case. A touch-hole is cut in and the butt end of the barrel stopped. The whole is lashed with string or wire to a wooden butt, often roughly carved to resemble a rifle stock. The wood for this stock again comes from a funeral bier, though there is less need of sympathetic magic. Only where a bullet case is used, is the touch-hole to be found at the base of the case rather than on the side; this type of barrel further varies by its not projecting beyond its stock. Beeswax frequently coats the gun and, if the barrel is a bullet case, masks it almost entirely. Often too, lucky beans (*Abrus precatorius*) are set in the beeswax. These bright red and black seeds (*mupitipiti*) are dangerous if crushed and then swallowed for they contain a tox-albumin, abrin, which is very poisonous. They are always associated with dangerous magic, not only in Barotseland and its environs but also in other parts of southern Africa.[1] When they are found decorating an object, it may with safety be identified as being used in sorcery, witchcraft or some such practice. Herbalism and other minor practices, such as elementary divining and the use of charms, do not normally have lucky beans in association with their equipment.

The gun is charged with gunpowder and medicated shot, which normally consists of finger bones, pieces of roots and other charmed objects. Some informants state that a piece of the clothing of the victim of the suspected *muloi's* attack is also included. The shot for a Luchazi gun was prepared as follows:

> you take the root of a tree named *muwewe* (?*Sterculia sp.*). You then take the outer part of this root and dry it. After drying you make it into a powder. Part of this root is made into two small pieces like bullets. After this preparation you put these two pieces into the barrel of the gun, you put a mixture of gunpowder and powdered *muwewe* root into the touch-hole of the *kaliloze* gun and you then fire....

The shot for another Luchazi gun was prepared in similar fashion, even to the two 'bullets' and mixing of powders in the touch-hole, but the root of the *mwinda* tree (*Securidaca longipedunculata*) was preferred to that of *muwewe*.

The choice of shot varies from case to case. Some *kaliloze* doctors prefer millet or sorghum seeds; others use nothing except gunpowder. In the modern *kaliloze*, however, preference is shown for

---

[1] Junod (1927.II.314) notes their usage among the Thonga of Portuguese East Africa. Drennan (1934.386) notes their usage in south-eastern Angola.

more physically satisfactory missiles, such as wire or fragments of copper or of other metal. Whereas the traditional weapons produced no wound and, as will be seen later, did not, except in the few cases where millet seed was used, even cause their contents to strike their victim, the modern guns with their lethal missiles do. In the three trials for murder held at Mongu, the medical evidence on the wounds caused by the *kaliloze* guns used was as follows:

External examination revealed 3 small wounds on the left side of the body just under the ribs about four inches from the spine, on the right side of the spine. . . . The large intestine was perforated. In the intestine I found one piece of metal. In the blood in the cavity I found one further piece of metal and one piece of hardwood. . . . On the assumption that the wounds caused the haemorrhage, death would have occurred not more than two hours after receiving the wounds. (Northern Rhodesia Government, 1957c.30–31.)

I found a wound one inch in diameter over the left shoulder blade—it had a ragged edge and would have been a group of wounds—it was putrefied. The shoulder blade was shattered.
. . . I found eight pieces of metal within the pleural cavity. A few of them were on top of the liver.
. . . One would not expect a person so injured to live without medical aid for more than five minutes. (Northern Rhodesia Government, 1957a.21–22.)

Ultimate cause of death was haemorrhage due to gunshot wounds which had entered the body below and behind the left armpit (indicated).
There were four wounds—holes in the skin—these were entrance wounds about $\frac{1}{4}''$ in diameter over an area of $3\frac{1}{2}/4$ inches in diameter. There were powder marks round the entrance wounds one being particularly marked. This indicated that the shot had been discharged at short range about 3–4 feet. I examined the body internally and found 4 pieces of metal in a position bearing a relationship to such wound. These pieces were in the chest cavity having penetrated beyond the chest wall, a depth of 1 to $1\frac{1}{2}$ inches.
. . . The wounds were gunshot wounds—metal fragments, and powder marks—charring and powder grains embedded in the skin. . . . The only powder that I can think of producing this sort of marking would be charcoal powder, blown into and penetrating the skin. (Northern Rhodesia Government, 1957b.2–3.)

Manner of Usage

Accounts of the pointing and discharge of the *kaliloze* gun vary in some details. Obviously, so far as the modern *kaliloze* is concerned, the only satisfactory direction is straight at the victim. Somili Mu-

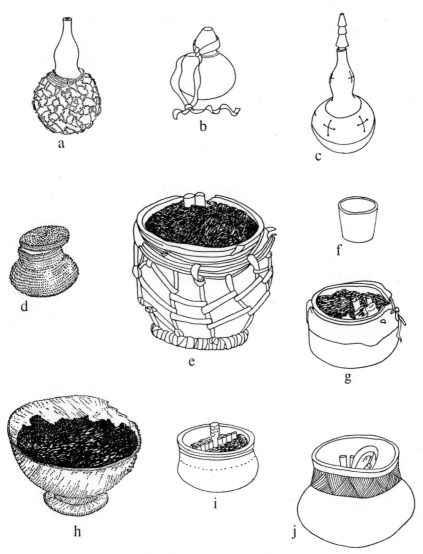

Fig. 15. Medicine containers (iii); various

a, b and c. Gourds   d and h. Baskets   e–g, i and j. Clay pots

yawa, a defendant in one of the cases quoted above, explained during his trial how he stood in the doorway of his victim's hut and lit the touch-hole with a match, saying the while, 'If you are a witch you must die tonight—but if you are not, you must not die.' (Northern Rhodesia Government, 1957a.56–57.) In other cases the gunman has been known to make a hole in the wall of the sleeping hut and to fire through it at his victim (White, 1948.100). Generally speaking, the need is for a close range and direct aim at the victim. As may be gathered from Muyawa's exhortation, the gunman puts more faith in *siposo* than in gunpowder.

With regard to the traditional *kaliloze*, White (ibid.) states, 'The night gun is pointed at the victim and when it is fired the victim dies. It is fired in the usual way by applying a match but no medicine actually touches the body of the victim, who nevertheless dies.' Some informants confirm this; others confirm only partially. Thus a Lozi doctor, who used sorghum and millet seed shot, said, '(when the gun is fired) the seed strikes the victim and also the smoke from the burning powder. Without this smoke the victim would not be bewitched. The victim generally wakes up when the seed strikes him and when he hears the noise. The next morning he feels sick and later dies.' An Nkoya informant who also used millet seed confirmed the essential facts of this account, particularly the importance of the smoke. The Luchazi gunman who preferred *muwewe* root and shot emphasized, 'You go as near as possible to your victim by crawling. You have to light a match before firing. The range of this gun is about 10 feet.' One *kaliloze* gun, the shot of which was made of wire, was fired at a woman in a forest garden : 'She fell but got up again and went home. Next morning she was dead.' As may be seen there is no evidence to show that the victim dies immediately on hearing the report of the gun.

There is another school of thought on this matter of direction. In this, it is held that there is no need to stalk or come close to the corporeal *muloi*. Indeed some would go so far as to claim that the name of the *muloi* need not even be known, the *kaliloze* missiles being selective. Doctors of this persuasion point and discharge their *kaliloze* at the sun, either because they believe the missiles will then seek out the appropriate *muloi*, whoever and wherever he or she may be, or because they believe that *baloi* congregate round the sun in the early morning. A Kwandi doctor, having fashioned a *kaliloze* out of wood, gave it to his client or apprentice with the instruction that he should point the gun at the sun and fire it by means of dried grass, picked off a much-frequented path and inserted in the touch-hole of the gun. The gun would then fire in any direction and would kill the *muloi*. In another case involving a Mashi doctor, the *kaliloze* was said to be fired at the rising sun, and the prayer made : 'before the sun sets the witch responsible . . . shall become ill and subsequently die from this illness, i.e. the kaliloze bullet.'

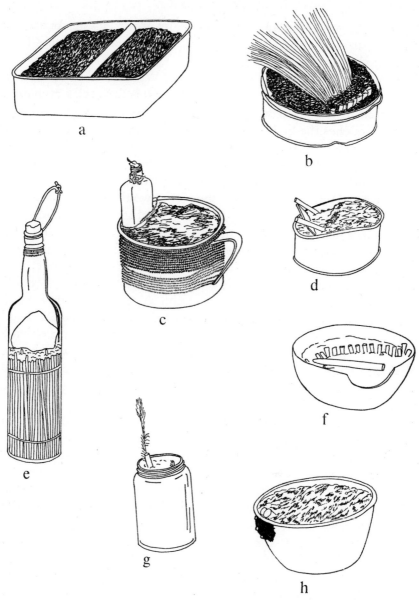

Fig. 16. Medicine containers (iv); various

a, b, d and h. Tins and enamel ware

c. Bottle set in a bead-covered tin cup

e and g. Bottles

f. Gourd

Kaliloze guns cannot be used by laymen, only by initiated doctors or gunmen. A man wishing to kill somebody with such a weapon must, therefore, employ one of these men. This is expensive and, to judge from the few records, the client either pays about five pounds in cash, or promises the doctor a cow. Usually a small down payment is required, the main part of the transaction being fulfilled on the successful conclusion of the murder.

Origins

It is unlikely that the modern *kaliloze* dates back further than some fifteen or twenty years, and 1942 has been suggested as the year in or about which it was introduced, though there is little evidence to confirm this. The traditional *kaliloze*, however, is known to have been used before that time. Even so, the whole idea of *kaliloze* cannot be very old, for the use of gunpowder must have been borrowed from European traders and explorers. These were, most probably, the Portuguese of Angola, for the *kaliloze*, so far as is known, is restricted in distribution to the LUNDA-LUVALE peoples and to those tribes with whom they have come into contact. The practice is not found among the tribes of Southern Rhodesia or of north-eastern Rhodesia. The increasing popularity of this weapon in recent years and its ready acceptance by non-LUNDA-LUVALE tribes may perhaps be due, as Lemon[1] suggests, to the discontinuation of the practice of destroying *baloi* by burning them. In Kalabo, such a punishment occurred as late as 1937. With witchcraft apparently on the increase and traditional methods of control forbidden, the inhabitants of Barotseland probably welcomed the 'new' weapon of retribution.

It is tempting to look for a fore-runner of the *kaliloze*. Where better than among the Bushmen? There are Bushman groups in south-eastern Angola, the Caprivi Strip, South-West Africa and Bechuanaland as well as a few bands in Sesheke district. Schapera (1930.199) notes that the Bushman love-bow, a small magic bow and arrows, is to be found among all north-western tribes, while Bleek (1928.28), speaking of the Naron Bushmen, says, 'A medicine man wishing to destroy another, comes up close and shoots at the opponent's kaross with one of these arrows, blunt end foremost. The missile falls harmlessly to the ground, but the victim dies of magic.'

It is feasible that the Bantu in this part of Africa borrowed and modified this practice from the Bushmen. The addition of a noisy

[1] Kalabo district files, 1958.

and vivid explosion must have done much to make the practice popular[1] among Bantu peoples.

The idea of magical destruction, by pointing or discharging a weapon at the victim, is not confined to Africa. The most famous parallel is the Australian Aborigine's pointing bone, the use of which is described by Rose (1957). The very commonness of this method of bewitching is an argument in favour of a precursor of the *kaliloze* gun and, while there is no obvious connecting link between magic gun and magic bow, one may reasonably postulate such a link. One Kwandi witchdoctor, tried at Senanga, had a most lethal collection of magic weapons of some significance in this context. He specialized in the execution of *baloi* rather than in the curing of patients and possessed, on arrest, one wooden and one human limb bone *kaliloze* gun, four human limb bones (raw material?), twelve *sikuyeti* sticks, a pot of reputedly human fat, and finally a curious bow and arrow termed a *kata* (diminutive of *wuta*-bow). The stave of the *kata* (Fig. 6(f)), which measures some six inches from end to end, is a child's rib bone[2]; the string is of sinew and the arrow is a small sliver of hardwood. Dangling from the bowstring is a fish-hook. The owner claimed that he had obtained the *kaliloze*, the human bones and the *kata* in September, 1956, from a Bushman in the Mashi valley. The price was one pound and the vendor promised to return and demonstrate the use of the *kata*. This promise, he said, was never kept. Both *kaliloze* and *kata* were claimed to be magic killers of *baloi*. They are fired either at the ground or at the sun.

From an examination of the *kata* it would appear to be either of Bushman origin or a copy of a Bushman weapon. The arrow is similar, even to the detachable blunt head. Only the use of the bone stave is unusual. If, therefore, it is accepted that the owner obtained *kaliloze*, bones, and *kata* from a Bushman, and there is no reason why he should not be believed for, being completely crippled, he would find great difficulty in collecting the bones himself from a grave, then this would indicate a connection between *kaliloze* and *kata*. Further than this, however, the argument cannot be pressed for there is no information available as to whether Bushmen use *kaliloze* guns.

---

[1] It is a curious coincidence that the Bushman love-bow should also be given the name of 'the Bushman revolver'.

[2] I am most grateful to Professor P. V. Tobias of the Department of Anatomy, the Medical School, the University of the Witwatersrand, for identifying this bone.

Fig. 17. Medicine containers (v); various

a, c and e. Bundles of medicinal roots and sticks; specimen a contained in a sisal bag
    resembling crochet work
b. Pressed cake
d. Cloth bag open to show some of its contents
f. Cloth bag
g. Bark cloth bag
h. Skin wrapper

87

It is reasonable to surmise that the modern lethal *kaliloze* originated somewhere outside Barotseland, most probably on the line of
rail or in a mining centre, for the creator of such a weapon would
need to be in reasonably close contact with a supply of discarded
lengths of metal tubing. Since there is such a large and regular movement of labour to and from Wankie, and more so to and from the
Witwatersrand, it is most probably in one of these places that the
first lethal *kaliloze* was made, or at least the idea conceived. The
labourer concerned must then have brought it back to Barotseland
where its efficiency and less insistent demands for magical compe-
tency on the part of the user soon made it very popular. Possibly its
entry was influenced by a connection with *siposo*,[1] but there is no evidence either for or against this theory.

SIKUYETI

The word, *sikuyeti*, may be derived from the verb, *kuyata* (LU-
YANA), 'to cut' or 'to split' or, in the case of pimples or boils, 'to
lance'. The object of the *sikuyeti* ritual is quite simple. It is to per-
suade, by invocation, the spirit of the dead man to avenge itself upon
the *muloi* who caused his death. The power that enables it to do this
comes from the contact of the *sikuyeti* charm with the clothing of the
deceased.

The *sikuyeti* charm (Fig. 6(d) and (e)) consists normally of two,
three or four pointed sticks, hollowed out in the centre to resemble
duiker horns. The relative suspecting witchcraft obtains a set of these
sticks from a *sikuyeti* doctor or, more frequently, employs him to act
on his behalf, and secretly collects a few wisps of grass from the roof
of each house in the village wherein he suspects the guilty *muloi* to
live. Some doctors, such as the Kwandi cripple mentioned above,
also required charcoal from every fire in the village. The doctor takes
the charms, the grass, coals if any, and a little clothing of the deceased into the bush (the Kwandi specified a hole under a tree). Lay-
ing two of the sticks on the ground, he takes the clothing and the
third stick together in his hand and invokes the spirit of the deceased
to vengeance. When his prayer is completed, he blows or rather
whistles across the open end of the stick[2] and lays it with its fellows,
the grass and the clothing. A small bird or animal trap is set nearby.

[1] Singleton-Fisher (1949.20) notes the belief that the sharp pains of pneumonia are caused by
kaliloze bullets.
[2] A common way of attracting the attention of the ancestral spirits.

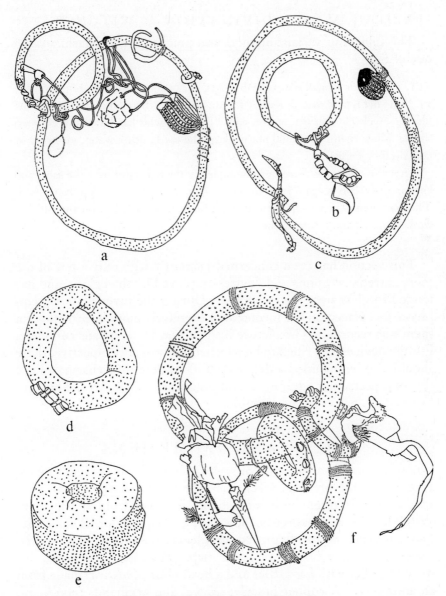

Fig. 18. Snake-skin belts and bracelets

This is based primarily on a Simaa account. The Kwandi doctor continued it by saying that, on the following day, the doctor returns and examines the trap. If it has caught anything, this indicates that the death was in fact the work of a *muloi*. The animal or bird is killed (the head being cut off) and the *muloi* dies a day or so later.

89

The following variant method was practised by a Mashi *sikuyeti* doctor :

The charm is a small net. Certain roots, sticks and medicines are put on the fire. The net is held over to receive the smoke and is then put on the face of the (doctor or client) and the prayer said. 'The one who has killed my children should follow them, he should not walk on the earth, drink water, eat bread or take snuff or smoke.'

After the sticks, etc. have burnt completely the net is put over the ashes and left for a day. Then again it is put on the face of the doctor. No prayer is said. The doctor must not sleep with his wife for four days. Then on the fifth he washes himself and returns to her.

This section has been concerned primarily with only a few of the more extreme weapons and devices employed by the *ng'aka*, and has tended to gloss over the remainder. During the investigations, emphasis was placed on the former and, therefore, more information on them was recorded. The picture is, however, by no means complete. For the devices described to be seen in their proper perspective, there should also be included a detailed study of defensive charms and of the less spectacular equipment and practices of the *ng'aka*. This, unfortunately, has not been possible.

DRESS AND EQUIPMENT

Unless he practices exorcism or seeks to impress his audience by his appearance, the ordinary leech has little need of a special costume and, in fact, is often indistinguishable in dress from the layman. Witchdoctors and exorcists, however, perhaps in order to excite their audience or to obtain its confidence, do usually don special dress. Skirts (*mashamba*) of bark strip, skins, grass or reeds, are worn together with leg-rattles and a head plume (*ndelwa*) made from an animal tail. A copper bracelet (*liseka*) and armbands (*muulu*, pl. *miulu*), especially of medicine-filled python skins are also worn, together with belts of a similar kind (Fig. 18). A headband (*silele*) may be used in place of the plume, while the shoulders are enhanced by the addition of fringes of zebra or wildebeeste mane (*likumbi*, pl. *makumbi*, dimin. *tukumbi*). Strings of beads and charms may also be worn round the neck, the waist or across the chest, while a bell (*mulangu*) or rattle (*mulai, musambo*) (Fig. 20) and flyswitch (*muhata*)

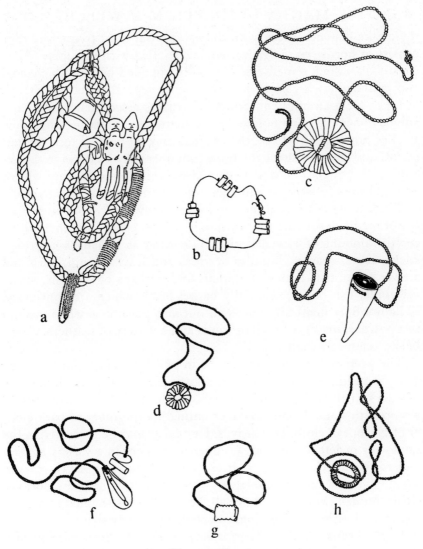

Fig. 19. Charms

a. Plaited bark strip belt
b–h. Various charms, all collected by the late Dr. K. Lepehne; specimen g has a sachet
of snakeskin

(Figs. 8, 9 and 10) are almost indispensable accessories. The handle
of the last-named usually contains medicines or charms.

While dancing, exorcizing or curing, the *ng'aka* usually protects
himself, the patient and the immediate area around them both from
magical attack, by setting up special defensive charms. The form

these take depends entirely on the *ng'aka*, but most frequently they consist of horns (*mushengo*, pl. *mishengo*) filled with medicine (Figs. 11 and 12). Such a medicine is usually obtained by mixing charred and pounded sticks, roots, leaves or other vegetable matter with oil or fat to form an unguent. Some informants assert that human and animal bones and other non-vegetable matter are sometimes included. Duiker horns or short lengths of stick may be pushed into the unguent, and the outside of the horn container may be decorated, perhaps with beads. The doctor may also, while he is dancing, throw around leaves (*nsompo*) as a further defence against magical attacks.

The kits of both herbal and witchdoctors invariably contain a number of medicines (using the word in its widest sense) together with a certain amount of raw material. The latter is usually vegetable—sticks, roots, grasses, bundles of vines and leaves, fungi, bark and seeds ; or animal—bones of animals and perhaps of humans, snake vertebrae, fish bones, especially barbel heads which are considered to be not only magically powerful but also poisonous when ground to a powder, insects of various kinds and a variety of feathers, claws, beaks, teeth and shells.

The prepared medicines[1] may be in powder form, solution, a dry cake or an unguent as described above. Liquids are kept in bottles, powders in tins, small jars, gourds, cloth or skin bags, or merely wrapped in a small skin (snake or animal), a fragment of bark cloth or of European cloth, or in leaves. Dry cakes may be protected in the same way or left uncovered. Unguents are kept in a variety of containers—small clay pots, bottles, enamel cups, gourds, carved wooden vessels such as miniature wooden mortars or boats, tortoise shells, human skulls and, above all, horns. The last-named may be of any animal, either wild or domesticated, and of any size.

Lucky beans (*Abrus precatorius*) have a very strong association with witchcraft and sorcery and are present in almost all witchcraft kits, usually decorating a witchfinding apparatus, skull, *kaliloze* gun or even the box or trunk itself that contains the kit.

One or more flyswitches should also be present, and the handles of these may be decorated with beads, skins, basketwork or cloth and contain an unguent and perhaps sticks, small horns or slivers of bone. Finally, each box may contain items peculiar to the craft of its owner—witchfinding devices for the witchdoctor, cupping horns for

---

[1] For the various containers see Figs. 11–18.

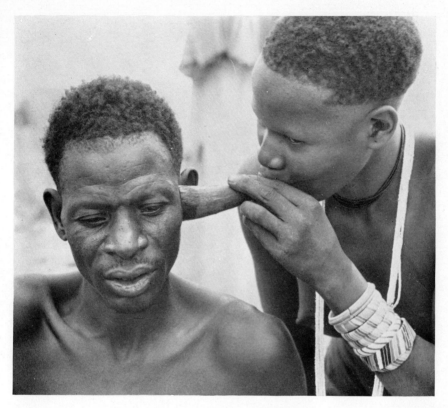

Cupping blood; applying the horn

Fig. 20. Rattles; cupping horns

a–d. Hand rattles; the body of specimen c is a modern tin
e. Cupping horns; three are of gourd and three of actual horn

the herbalist, and also pieces of chalk with which to mark the patient and perhaps the doctor himself during treatment.

This chapter represents an attempt not only to describe the maladies, both medical and magical, that the *ng'aka* treats and the methods and equipment he employs, but also to explain his role in society. The *ng'aka* cannot be considered separately from the society in which he lives for he is not, as is often thought, a parasite growing rich on the fears and misfortunes of his neighbours. He does a considerable amount of good by curing, as best he can, actual physical ailments, by treating psychical disorders and by assisting the other members of the community in their dealings with the supernatural world. The *ng'aka* is a responsible and highly respected member of this community. Without him central African society is incomplete, for he fills a very real need. There is much that the ordinary villager cannot understand, so many inexplicable misfortunes that occur suddenly, without warning, to cause him distress or suffering. The diviner comforts by indicating a possible cause of such misfortunes ; the *ng'aka* helps by providing a means of controlling the supernatural and, where witchcraft is indicated, of obtaining revenge.

The changes brought about by contact with the outside world have not reduced the African's fear of the unknown ; rather they have, in many cases, by undermining his traditional beliefs and values, increased these fears and made him yet more uncertain. As a result, the *ng'aka* is even more in demand though he has been compelled, as has been shown, to modernize his methods and to learn to treat many new and foreign maladies in order to keep pace with this demand.

CHAPTER IV

THE *MULAULI*

Ng'aka and *muloi*, friend and foe. To the layman, these must appear as the most important figures on the battlefield of magic. Yet there is a third that overshadows them both, without whose intervention the *muloi* would remain undiscovered and the *ng'aka* be impotent. This is the diviner, *mulauli*. He it is who enables the *ng'aka* to establish contact with the *muloi* and, on a lower plane, sends the *ng'aka* his clients. Without the diviner, in fact, belief in magic and in the supernatural would lose much of its strength, for it is he who continually demonstrates its importance in the affairs of ordinary people.

Divination is defined in the *Shorter Oxford English Dictionary* as, 'the foretelling of future events or discovery of what is hidden or obscure by supernatural or magical means.' Accordingly, there are described later in this chapter not only those methods that are normally considered under the heading of divining practices, but also such practices as the smelling out of cannibals and necrophagers, the diagnosis of sickness by the manner of the patient's reaction to treatment, and *kaliloze* and *sikuyeti* selection of offending sorcerers.

Divining and witchfinding are often considered as though they were separate practices, the one harmless the other evil. In actual fact, however, they are not separate and can, and indeed often are carried on by the same person. The only difference lies in the degree of skill of the diviner concerned; for just as the witchdoctor is a specialist *ng'aka*, so the witchfinder is a specialist *mulauli*. Again, the same vernacular name is given to both witchfinder and diviner. There is further specialization among diviners based not only on experience, but also on preference for particular ailments. This is very common where the diviner is also a doctor.

Since the only real test of a diviner is of his ability to attract clients, there exist many mediocre practitioners[1] whose intelligence and experience leave much to be desired. On the other hand, there are a number who are intelligent, highly skilled and, as a result, very successful. Kuntz (1932.134) points out that such *'grands divins'* prac-

---

[1] These probably account for a considerable part of the high proportion of diviners noted in Chapter VII.

tise *'la divination mentale'* without the aid of mechanical devices. This has been confirmed during the present study.

The Diagnosis

In a divination the answers a diviner can give are limited. Should the consultation be about the future and a project planned by the client, then the answer will obviously be closely related to that project. Should the consultation be about the cause of misfortune, sickness or death, then the diviner must diagnose interference by one of the following :

a *muloi* ;
an *ng'aka* because the victim is a *muloi* ;
another person by means of a charm (for example, if the victim has been committing adultery with his wife) ;
bush spirits ;
ancestral spirits ;

or

no supernatural interference, the cause being purely rational ;
he can instead admit failure and send his client elsewhere, but this is not common ; if the client feels he is getting nowhere he will himself terminate the consultation.

After this primary diagnosis, throughout the whole of which he has been assisted by the clients who indicate, at each stage in the proceedings, how 'warm' or 'cold' are his diagnoses, the diviner proceeds to narrow the field :

by indicating the *muloi* responsible, usually by circumlocution and reference to the social or kinship position or relationship he holds. Occasionally, the diviner may quite baldly accuse him by name.[1] The diviner may also suggest lines of defence and treatment if requested ;
by finding the *ng'aka* responsible, and persuading the suspected *muloi* to call off his own attacks. When this is done the *ng'aka* will then cease his ;
by finding the attacker and persuading him to call off the attack, or at least to provide the antidote. The doctor can often provide this himself ;

[1] As did, for example, the Totela diviner whose letter has already been quoted in Chapter II.

by finding the particular spirit responsible. Since each spirit usually causes but one kind of illness, the cure is then easily found or at least proposed ;

by finding the offended ancestor and the cause of his displeasure, and instructing the client accordingly how to placate and atone.

Considerable importance is attached to the diviner's ability to diagnose correctly. He is approached by relatives of the patient, not by the patient himself, and is first required to divine the reason for the visit. If he can do this successfully he is allowed to continue and to diagnose the cause of the ailment. If he cannot, the clients pick up their money and go elsewhere. Even if he is successful and not only diagnoses the cause of the trouble but also suggests a remedy, he does not receive his full fee. He is given his initial fee, usually a small sum—threepence, sixpence, or one shilling—for the actual divination, but the main payment of ten shillings, one pound or an ox is not made until the cure has proved to be successful. In very serious cases, the charges are, of course, higher.

Associated Practices and Specialization

As may be gathered from the above discussion, not all diviners restrict themselves purely to divining. A considerable number combine their divining with herbal doctoring, a wise practice since the one usually leads to the other. Witchfinders too often combine their work with witchdoctoring. Similarly witchfinders, whether or not they are witchdoctors, often make routine divinations and may even indulge in herbal doctoring.

On the other hand, many diviners specialize. Thus we find some who confine themselves to a very few ailments. The *kaliloze* and *sikuyeti* doctors are examples of these. Yet other diviners seek to broaden their knowledge in order to be able to recognize and diagnose more and more maladies. In recent years, as was explained in Chapter III, a number have allowed needles to be inserted in their bodies so that they might have the power to divine *siposo*.

Foreign Influences

Factors which affect the *ng'aka* similarly affect the *mulauli*. The craving, on the part of clients, for new and more satisfactory methods has, over the years, produced a whole crop of innovations and inventions in the divining field. Similarly, the exotic foreigner or foreign

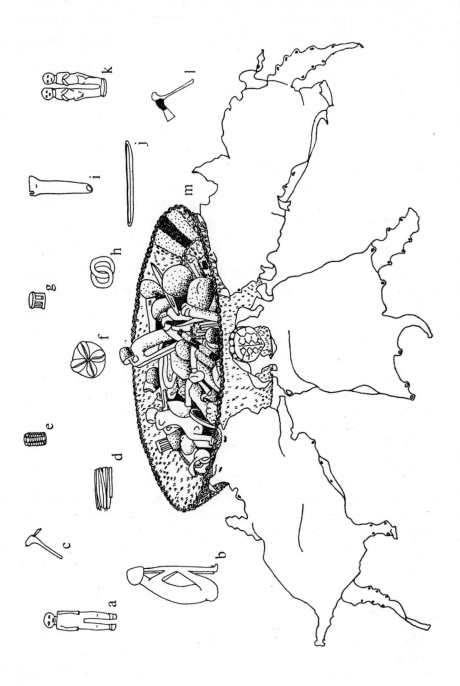

method has always found a ready clientele. It is interesting to note the frequency with which acculturation occurs and the wide diffusion of particular methods of known origin, such as divining bones and divining baskets, as well as the number of diviners who are either itinerant or who have in the past travelled abroad, for example to the Congo, to improve their knowledge.

The Diviner and Society

Much has been written on the position of the diviner in a society and on the way in which he is so often able to provide a solution acceptable both to his clients as individuals and to society as a whole. Obviously, a thorough knowledge of local events, combined with considerable experience of similar problems, a quick intuition and a convincing manner, are all highly necessary for a diviner to rise and to maintain his position. When dealing with illness, the diviner must further be so fully acquainted with the symptoms of different maladies that he is able to diagnose without seeing the patient, although no doubt he will have found it politic to learn something about the patient in question by more rational means. In fact, one might summarize the position of the diviner as standing with his fingers pressed, firmly but unobtrusively, upon the pulse of the society around him.

In what way, however, does an itinerant diviner diagnose sucessfully in a strange area? How can a diviner, consulted by a deputation from a village over a hundred miles away in a neighbouring district, achieve satisfactory results? The only feasible explanation is that

---

Fig. 21. Divining devices (i); the divining basket

a–l. Some of the symbols common to most baskets:

a and b. Figurines
c. Hoe
d. Case of the bag-worm (*Psychidae* moth)
e. Plaited palm leaf strip
f. Cowrie shells on a leather disc
g. Stool
h. Interlocking rings of wood
i. Drum
j. Canoe
k. Double figurine
l. Axe
m. Divining basket and contents. Note the red and white bars marked on the inner wall and the small tortoise shell and skins attached to the outside

informants are used, either from the troubled village or, more probably, from the nearby rest camp wherein the travellers, waiting for
the diviner to receive them, are liable in an unguarded moment to
divulge the reason for their visit. An itinerant may similarly possess
informants who provide him with the necessary details; perhaps
local diviners, out of professional loyalty, give him this data and are
allowed to associate with him at the divination, thus rubbing off
some of his prestige on to their own shoulders. This, however, is
mere conjecture.

DIVINING METHODS

For convenience, the methods described below have been grouped
under sub-headings. This arrangement is purely arbitrary, although
many of the methods are amenable to such grouping. Some, as will
be obvious, are not.

Many methods require symbols for good and evil. These are
usually represented by pieces or marks of white chalk and red ochre
respectively.

PATTERN

By pattern divination is meant the use of a number of material symbols which, being shaken together and cast on the ground, provide
answers by the positions they take up relative not only to each other
but also to some outside factor or factors.

The Divining Basket—ngombo yakusekula (Fig. 21)

The *ngombo* basket is one of the most interesting and, at the same
time, one of the most intricate of pattern, and for that matter of all
divining methods. Its full name is *ngombo yakusekula* (*kusekula*—'to
shake up'; *ngombo* is the generic L U N D A-L U V A L E term for any divining device) and it consists of a shallow winnowing basket,[1] some
three to six inches deep and about twelve inches wide at the rim,
which is broader than the base. This basket contains anything up to
a hundred or more symbols which, between them, represent all aspects of village and tribal life. The diviner tosses the basket up and
down, some three or four times, until he is satisfied that a pattern is
established on the surface of the contents. This pattern provides the

---

[1] As Turner (1961.5) points out, 'The winnowing basket itself stands for the sifting of
truth from falsehood.' The diviner also agitates the symbols in his divining basket in much the
same way as a woman agitates the grain in her winnowing basket.

divination. Thus, in the case of a sick man, the figurine representing him will, by its position, indicate whether he will die or be cured. When the cause of the illness is sought, the appropriate symbol will be found in juxtaposition to the main figurine. Similarly, when the nature of the malady is to be diagnosed, it is found by the juxtaposition of the figurine and the symbol representing that particular malady. As a corollary, the cure is indicated by the presence of the symbol representing it.

Obviously, where the name of a sorcerer is sought, the basket is not large enough to contain symbols for all known persons. However, the diviner narrows down the field to one suspect, standing in some particular relationship, either kinship or social, to the victim. No name need be given. Where the client is enquiring about some project he is about to undertake, the same general principles apply. If the canoe symbol is thrown upside down, the dangers of the proposed journey are obvious and so on.

This is necessarily a brief sketch of the meanings of the symbols and it is to be emphasized that few symbols are restricted to one meaning alone. Thus, for example, the 'canoe' represents not only a boat, water journey, land journey and fishing, but also a particular disease known as *nzila* ('a path'). Each symbol has shades of meaning appropriate to the particular divination, and its position in relation to other symbols affects these. Even its absence may be of importance.

On examining a number of baskets, it is possible to find considerable agreement between their contents, for many of the symbols are identical in form. Not all of these, however, hold identical meanings. Obviously, certain main items must mean the same to all diviners, but balls of beeswax, containing a tiny fragment of root or a coin, cannot be so easily identified, for such symbols are created by the owner of that particular basket and hold a meaning for him alone. For example, early in his career a diviner/doctor diagnoses a particular malady and treats it successfully. This is the first time he has been required to deal with this complaint, or perhaps this is the first of the many cures he has tried which succeeds. He, therefore, takes a symbol, a fragment of the root used in the medicine, a curl of the patient's hair or a coin from this first payment, and sets it in a small ball of beeswax. At subsequent divinations, when this ball appears in his basket, he can confidently give both diagnosis and cure. Another diviner/doctor may create a similar symbol by the same method, but it would represent for him an entirely different sickness and/or cure.

One cannot, therefore, discover the meanings of all the symbols in a basket without recourse to and the honest co-operation of the owner of that particular basket.

Very little work has as yet been done on this subject.[1] Delachaux's (1946) paper is both interesting and useful but it is based on a very few baskets collected over a very wide area. Further, of the contents of the Chokwe basket which he describes in detail, neither he nor Berger, who collected the basket, were able to identify more than 23 of the 205 objects.

In Northern Rhodesia, the *ngombo* basket is only found, except in isolated instances, among the LUNDA-LUVALE of the west and north-west. Its distribution through Angola and the southern Congo must be very wide, but there is comparatively little data available on the divining practices of the tribes of these territories. In Barotseland and in other parts of Northern Rhodesia, immigrant LUNDA-LUVALE have a considerable influence on almost all aspects of indigenous material culture, notably in the field of magic. It is, therefore, not surprising to find a number of diviners from other tribes and groups copying, with varying success, this most difficult of practices.

The training of an *ngombo* basket diviner must be both difficult and arduous. No doubt it is also expensive. An interesting point about this training is that the novice must first kill a near relative before his basket is able to function properly, a most unusual requirement of a diviner, and one which shows the respect with which this particular device is regarded.

While some *ngombo* diviners restrict themselves to the one method, others employ alternative methods of a simpler nature. These are described below.

Divining Bones—makakata (Fig. 22)

While basket divining is probably the most interesting of divining methods, the most widely known and the most popular in southern Africa is that of 'throwing the bones'. This phrase is frequently mis-applied to all kinds of processes. It should, however, only be used where symbols of bone, ivory, horn or wood, usually carved or decorated, are gathered in the hands or in a container and cast down together, on the ground or on some flat surface, to form the pattern on which the diviner may base his diagnosis.

[1] Since this was written, Turner's (1961) study of Ndembu divining baskets and their contents has been published.

Fig. 22. Divining devices (ii); divining bones

a. Plateau Tonga *makakata*
b. Mashona *hakata*
c and e. Barotse *makakata*; simple sets
d. Masarwa *makakata*
f. *Mungongo (Ricinodendron rautenenii)* nutshell *makakata*
g. Venda astraguli
h. Barotse *makakata*; complex set

Divining bones are widely used south of the Zambezi though they are, or were until recent years, only to be found among the Sotho, the Venda, and the Shangana-Tonga. The Nguni tribes preferred their witches to be 'smelt out' by *isanusi*, and their diviners to practise mental divination (Hoernlé, 1937.235–240).

To the north of the Zambezi, divining bones have only been observed in Barotseland and among the Ila and the Plateau and Valley Tonga though doubtless, with rapidly improving communications and increasing opportunities for travel, they are being adopted by other peoples.

In East Africa, comparable methods are employed. The Bantu Kavirondo diviner, for example, uses pebbles :

shaking the pebbles between the palms of his hands. If a pebble drops from his hand on the hide while he is uttering one of these words, the particular object, person, ancestral spirit, or whatever other agent the word signifies has thereby been detected as the cause of the illness. . . .

An alternative technique of handling the pebbles oracle consists of letting all the pebbles drop on the hide whenever a new potential cause is named. In that case the answer is supplied if one pebble comes to lie apart from the others. (Wagner, 1949.227.)

On the Tanganyika Plateau, a similar method is used :

divination with the bones, which are dealt out in two while the names of the suspects are repeated, until finally an odd bone is dealt out by sleight of hand at the name of the erring spirit, has been so frequently described among central African tribes as to require no further notice. (Gouldsbury and Sheane, 1911. 89.)

Neither of these devices are really sets of divining bones in the sense of their comprising individual symbols that, on being thrown down, provide a pattern for diagnosis.

The tribes to the north and north-west of Barotseland do not apparently possess divining bones, and there is no record of their usage among LUNDA-LUVALE, except where there has been definite contact with LUYANA or other groups. The device is essentially southern African both in distribution and origin. Since its usage by Bushmen is limited to those groups that have been exposed to strong Bantu influence (Schapera, 1930.200–201), it is almost certainly of Bantu origin.

It is possible to distinguish several varieties of divining bones :

ASTRAGULI (Fig. 22(g)). These are very common among the Venda and the Shangana-Tonga. Junod's (1927.II.541–564) excellent analysis of such a set is undoubtedly the best of its kind ever attempted. Kuntz (1932.133–134) observed the use of knucklebones (*osselets*) in Barotseland but, nowadays at least, they are rarely to be found in the Protectorate.

WOODEN TABLETS–*hakata* (Fig. 22(b)). These carved and rather large wooden 'bones', which are Shona in origin though they have also been adopted by the Ndebele, have attracted a considerable amount of attention.[1] Their distribution, however, appears to be limited to Southern Rhodesia and no report of their use in Barotseland, or in any area north of the Zambezi, has been recorded, though there is an interesting similarity of decoration with a Plateau Tonga set of *makakata* tablets in the collections of the Rhodes-Livingstone Museum (Fig. 22(a)).

According to Tracey (1934.23) the *hakata* are not necessarily of wood : 'There are still a few sets to be found of bone and ivory, but mostly in private collections, for whenever they were discovered by the authorities they were confiscated.'

BONE TABLETS–*makakata*.[2] This type of divining bone has a wide distribution and is commonly found not only in Northern Rhodesia, but also among southern tribes, such as the Bechuana and the Pedi (Junod, 1927.II.603–608). The tablets, which may be either of ivory or of actual bone,[3] are usually decorated, though only on one side. While this decoration appears to vary but little, the shapes of the tablets themselves vary to an interesting degree. Among the Pedi and, it would seem, among many tribes south of the Zambezi, the tablet is oblong, and a V-shaped notch is cut at one end. North of the Zambezi, this notch is not found : The tablets are much narrower and longer and, by means of a step cut into each side close to one end, the impression of a head is created (Fig. 22(c), (e) and (h)). Garbutt (1909.539) considers that this type of tablet is evidently intended

[1] For example, Tracey (1934), Hunt (1950) and Gelfand (1956). Gelfand devotes a complete chapter to the *hakata*.

[2] Cf. the terms, *hakata* (Mashona bones) and *hakati* (Shangana-Tonga divining nutshells). Often, in Barotseland, the term, *litaula*, normally applicable to any divining device, is used as a synonym for *makakata*. Hoernlé (1937.238) notes that Sotho divining bones (tablets, etc.) are known as *ditaolo* (some Bantu-speaking peoples find difficulty in pronouncing 'l' and replace it by 'd').

[3] Wooden replicas (Fig. 22(a)) may also be used, but are obviously copies of the true bones and intended to be used in conjunction with them. They are in no way similar to the wooden *hakata* of the Shona.

to be fish-shaped. There is, however, no evidence to support this theory.

The distribution of the notched tablet is very wide, and specimens have been collected[1] from as far north as north-east Bechuanaland (Fig. 22(d)) yet, of twenty-three Barotse and Plateau Tonga sets in the Rhodes-Livingstone Museum collections, none were of the notched variety. Although no Ila sets have been examined, Smith and Dale's (1920.I.272) note (which is the only reference to the use of divining bones by the Ila), 'We have known one or two diviners who used the *Makakata*, the divining bones, but as they are not native to the Ba-ila but were introduced probably from the Barotsi . . . ,' is assumed, especially since the LUYANA term, *makakata*, is employed, to refer to the headed (Barotse) variety. The Tonga probably obtained theirs from the same source.

Makakata would appear to be well-established in southern Barotseland and in the plain. Here, they are widely used and there is no hint of their being a recent innovation. Neither is it likely that the device was independently invented in Barotseland. Its limited diffusion, the similarity of name, of general shape, of decoration, of size of sets and, most important, of basis and method of interpretation, indicate links with the South-Eastern Bantu and to its arrival in Barotseland some generations ago, probably with the Kololo, who were principally of Sotho origin. If the device had been borrowed from neighbours living on the southern border, it would be most unlikely that the shape would have changed so markedly from the notched to the headed variety. It is more reasonable to suppose that once the device had been introduced, there was little continued contact with other tribes using divining tablets. During the nineteenth century, such would have been the case, for the Kololo and Barotse, because of Ndebele hostility, had few contacts with the south. It would have been quite simple for local variation to occur unchecked, especially after the destruction of the Kololo.

There are really two kinds of Barotse tablet sets. The first and less variable (Fig. 22(a), (c) and (e)) consists of a restricted number, usually four, of carved symbols which, being of the same material and being carved and marked on one surface only, differ but slightly one from the other. These markings, which are cut or burnt into the tablet and are spaced irregularly and apparently haphazardly over

[1] From a group of Masarwa, by the writer, 1955.

the surface, almost always take the form of small circles with a dot in the centre. The meaning of and reason for this type of decoration are unknown. Perhaps they may be fertility symbols representing a woman's breasts, or even eyes to assist the diviner. They could just as easily be meaningless patterns.[1] In such a set, each tablet has its own name and character which is adapted to suit the needs of the particular divination. For example, the set may consist of *father*, *wife*, *son* and *son's wife*. A lost cow would be represented by the *wife* tablet ; a calf by the sexually appropriate *son* or *son's wife* tablet. The pattern is created by the position of the tablets in relation to the ground, face up or down, to direction and to each other. Some tablets are so carved as to have differently shaped or marked ends ; such double-ended tablets enable a more detailed pattern to be produced.

The second kind of tablet set is much less formal (Fig. 22(h)). It contains a varied assortment of bone tablets, together with a few sticks or other extraneous items, such as coins, buttons or European poker dice, for good measure. The tablets themselves may or may not be carved and may be as many as fifteen or twenty in number. They may be single or double-ended. The general principles of pattern are the same although, by reason of the large number of symbols used, one is tempted to make comparisons with the *ngombo* basket method.

SEEDS AND NUT-SHELLS—*makakata* (Fig. 22(f)).[2] In Barotseland, these are almost invariably the nut-shells of the *mungongo* tree (*Ricinodendron rautenenii*) which have been split in half. It seems to be a pre-requisite that the nuts should have passed through the stomach of an elephant. A few such split shells are commonly included in the larger sets of bone tablets (Fig. 22(h)) but, where they are used on their own for divination, they may number as many as fifteen. As Gelfand (1956.116) points out, divining seeds are not strictly divining bones. The Barotse, however, closely associate the two, calling them both *makakata*.

These divining nuts are thrown in the same way as are tablets, and the answer is read from the pattern the half *mungongo* nuts, which resemble a walnut in shape, form in relation to the ground and to each other.

---

[1] See Segy (1953) for a discussion of the circle-dot symbol, its meaning and wide distribution.

[2] Known as *kakati* by the Shangana-Tonga (Hoernlé, 1937.236). Gelfand (1956.116) notes that the *mukakata* seeds used by the Shona are frequently referred to as *hakata*.

Whilst divining bones, to use the blanket term, can be and are used for all forms of divining and even witchfinding, two points are very noticeable. Firstly, perhaps because they are simple to use yet capable of providing something more than a 'Yes/No' divination, they are the most commonly used forms of divining, and are to be found in the possession of many otherwise ordinary people. At a consultation, there is no solemn ritual, such as often accompanies the consultation of the *ngombo* basket and other devices, nor is one given the impression that the user is a professional diviner.

Secondly, possibly because of the first point, there appears to be a strong link between herbal doctoring and bone-throwing. Exorcists and other doctors employing the more extreme anti-witchcraft methods rarely use divining bones, preferring LUNDA-LUVALE devices.

To conclude this section on pattern divining, it may be added that whereas bone divining is occasionally practised by women, basket divining is a purely male occupation. Further, as has been already indicated, basket divining is of much more importance than is bone-throwing in that men take it up seriously as a profession. No diviner was noted as practising both basket and bone pattern divining.

POINTING

The methods described in this and subsequent sections are all simple 'Yes/No' types which indicate by pointing either at one of two symbols or, in cases of witchfinding, directly at the suspect. Such symbols are commonly fragments of or marks made by red ochre and white chalk ; these represent evil and good respectively. When seeking a sorcerer, these symbols may be replaced by others, similar to the European sword and distaff, to represent both sides of the family.

Mat—kashasha (Fig. 23(b))

This consists of a miniature mat, some six to nine inches wide and some eighteen inches or more in length. The mat is folded in half lengthwise, and the strips forming the fold are tied in that position. On the distal strips of reed beeswax, with white beads or lucky beans impressed, may be smeared. For divining, the mat is opened out and held on edge at the fold so that the loose ends, which point in opposite directions, are allowed to swing freely. An affirmative answer causes the mat to go rigid and straight. Gelfand (1956.173) records the use of a similar divining mat by the Shona :

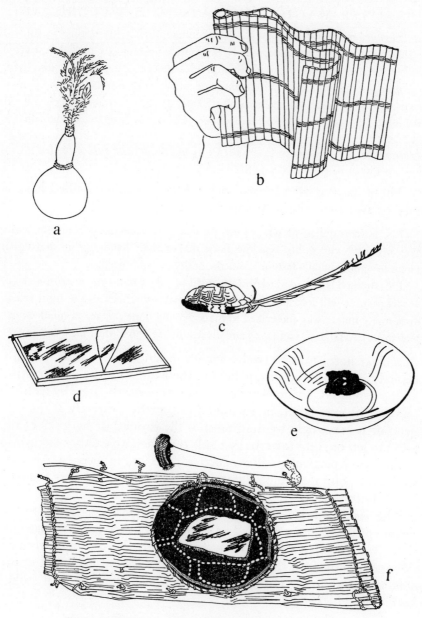

Fig. 23. Divining devices (iii); pointing and reflecting

a. Balancing gourd   c. Creeping tortoise
b. Mat   d, e and f. Mirrors, actual and otherwise

A *nganga* practising amongst the Vatavara employs an interesting instrument called his *ingere* for this purpose. It is simply a rectangular reed mat, twelve inches long and four inches wide, which folds easily. Sitting opposite his client, the *nganga* holds his *ingere* in his right hand and a horn from the wild pig (*indiri*) in his left. He chants, 'If you are going to die, come, I want to see you roll.' If the mat remains flat the patient will recover, but if it folds upon itself he will die.

Horn or Stick—sikunkula (LUYANA; *ngombo yakakundukundu* (LUNDA-LUVALE) (White, 1948b)[1]

These may be used in two ways: A large medicine-filled horn is held by two men (not including the diviner):

The horn is quiescent when they are near any innocent person, but when they approach the guilty one the horn makes their hands go up and down violently (pump handle fashion) over the guilty person's head. . . .

This method is also used to find the spirit of a dead man who is causing death or sickness. It will lead the people holding down the horn to the right grave, even many miles away (described to me as having done this for as much as sixteen miles). (Melland, 1923.225 and illustration at 176 of the *chilolo* device.)

A smaller horn, nine to twelve inches in length, or a stick, roughly carved to resemble a horn, is held in the hand with the point resting on the ground. Questions are posed and replies are given by its mute reaction. It may point, in a witchfinding matter, directly at the suspect, or it may reply by digging into the ground or by jerks of the point to left or right towards symbols representative either of kinship groups or of particular values, such as guilt and innocence. Alternatively, the point may remain stationary, and positive answers be given by the butt moving from side to side.

The smaller version of *sikunkula* is traditionally ascribed to the people of the Barotse plain. The larger has a very general distribution. One peculiar form of horn was collected at Senanga from an Mbunda diviner. In the mouth was fitted a carved head and upper shoulders and, in the crown of the head, was inserted a small duiker horn (Fig. 3(d)).

Creeping Tortoise—ngombo yakapeza (Fig. 23(c))

This is a LUNDA-LUVALE device often found in association with *ngombo* baskets. The *ngombo* basket, being so very complex, demands

---

[1] In this chapter, all subsequent references to White refer to this article unless otherwise indicated.

clear light for correct reading of its contents. Where divination is by lamplight or firelight, the diviner resorts to the simpler yet more dramatic tortoise. This is a small medicine-filled tortoise or turtle-shell into one orifice of which the feather of a vulture or, according to White, of a guinea-fowl has been inserted. By the direction this magical little tortoise takes on the ground, the diviner is able to provide the solution. The direction of movement may be towards a member of the audience or towards a symbol. The diviner meanwhile keeps contact by placing his fingers or hand on the tip of the feather. The balance is such that an inconspicuous downward pressure, with the heel of the hand on the tip of the feather, is enough to raise the shell on one end and, by a slight sideways motion, to move it forward. In the semi-darkness round a flickering fire, an audience would have great difficulty in deciding which was the cause and which the effect of movement.

Balanced Gourd (Fig. 23(a))

Finally, in this group, is the method of divining by balancing on the hand an unstable object, such as a small gourd, and letting it fall. The direction in which it points provides the answer. The medicine which fills the gourd acts also as ballast.

Berger (Delachaux, 1946.46) noted an axe used for a similar purpose, presumably by the Chokwe. The butt was set in the sand so that the axe stood straight, and the diviners danced round it until it fell. Conclusions were drawn from the marks it left in the sand and also by the direction of the fall.

There is no indication that the Lamba method of divining by lots, described by Doke (1931.282–284), is used in Barotseland. Three little sticks (*ifipa*), balanced close to a hole indicate, by remaining erect for a specified period or by falling into the hole, the answer to the question.

REVOLVING

Like pointing methods, the following indicate their answer by movement towards symbols. The difference is that they revolve on an axis and that the direction and speed of their movement provide the reply.

Ngombo Ya Kakolokolo (Fig. 25(c), (d) and (e))

This is described by White as follows :

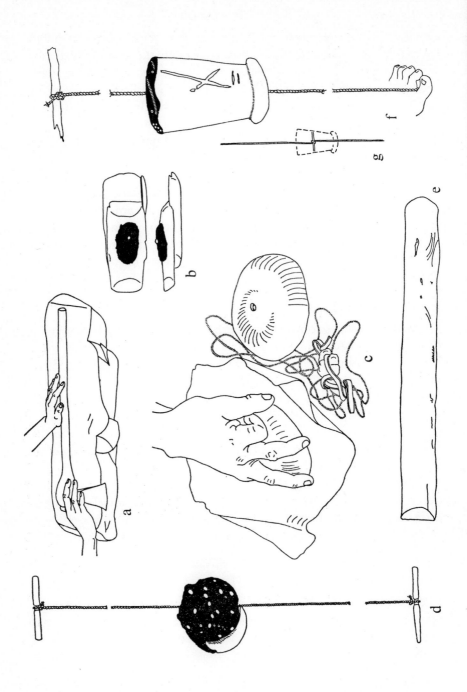

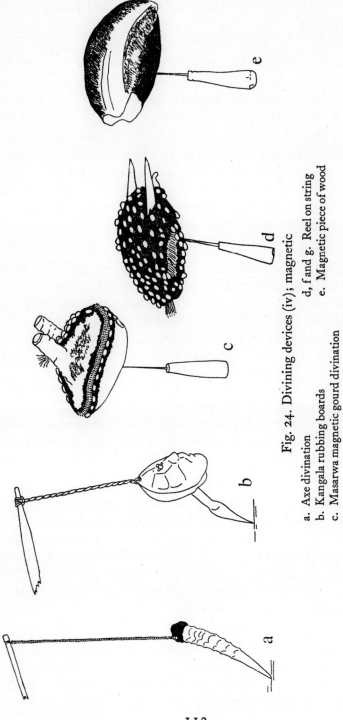

Fig. 24. Divining devices (iv); magnetic

a. Axe divination
b. Kangala rubbing boards
c. Masarwa magnetic gourd divination

d, f and g. Reel on string
e. Magnetic piece of wood

Fig. 25. Divining devices (v); revolving

a and b. *Ngombo yambinga*

c, d and e. *Ngombo ya kakolokolo*

Ngombo Ya Kakolokolo

This consists of the skull of a duiker adorned with bright scarlet seeds (*jiken-yenge*), and marked with white clay on the left side and with red clay on the right side. It is balanced on a sharp metal spike or nail and made to revolve as the names are called. If it revolves in the left-handed direction, i.e. that of the white clay, the name is blameless, whilst if in the direction of the red clay the guilty name is indicated.

The scarlet seeds mentioned are lucky beans and are set in beeswax. There is a variant form of the *kakolokolo* in which no red or white marks are applied to the skull, but red and white symbols are laid alongside and the skull circles on its spike in the appropriate direction.

This device was also observed by Kuntz (1932.133).

Ngombo Yambinga

A medicine-filled duiker horn is attached, at one side of its mouth, to a short string which in turn is tied to the end of a small twig, fishing rod fashion (Fig. 25(a)). The diviner holds the twig so that the point of the horn just touches the ground and takes the weight of the horn. Answers are given by the direction, clockwise or anti-clockwise, in which the butt of the horn circles on its point, and by the speed at which it so circles. (White)

Both Melland (1923.227–228, *kaneng'eni*) and Berger (Delachaux, 1946.46) observed this device.

A variant is a very small medicine-filled turtle or tortoise shell into one orifice of which a stick is inserted (Fig. 25(b)). The point of this stick rests on the ground and the method is the same as for the horn.

MAGNETIC

This form of divining has been noted in many parts of Africa, notably by Evans-Pritchard (1937) among the Azande where it takes the form of a rubbing stool. Whilst the rubbing stool does not occur in south-central Africa there are a number of similar and allied forms. The principle is that an object, which normally moves freely when rubbed on a flat surface, will stick and be temporarily immovable in answer to questions put by a diviner.

Axe—mufinyani (Fig. 24(a))

This is one of the commonest methods of friction divination and is to be found among many south-central African peoples, for example the Tonga and Shona, as well as in Barotseland. The axe, which is an ordinary working axe, consists of a wedge-shaped piece of iron tang-hafted in the bulbous head of a normal wooden handle. The axe is laid on its side, on the ground or on the back of a grind-stone, is held by the diviner at the head of the haft, and is slid gently forwards and backwards while he poses the question. The answer is indicated by its refusal to move in response to the pressure of his hand. The diviner taps it with his knuckles thereby releasing it, and a second question is then posed.

This method was observed among the Lamba by Doke (1931. 271–272) and among the Kaonde by Melland (1923.227, *kansheku*). The latter notes that it is employed only to divine troublesome an-cestral spirits.

Where an axe handle alone is used the method is the same, the movement being in a line parallel to the shaft.

Pestle—*munsi* (LUYANA) ; *ngombo yamwishi* (LUNDA-LUVALE)

This is an ordinary pounding pestle taken for the occasion. It is commonly used by LUNDA-LUVALE peoples and others, and the method is the same as that for the axe.

Alternatives to the pestle are pieces of wood (Fig. 24(e)) or, more often, the back of a wooden spoon. As White points out, 'among the Lunda and their allies a pounding stick is the more usual . . . (but) apparently any piece of wood can be used at a pinch.'

Rubbing Boards (Fig. 24(b))

The method that bears the closest resemblance to the Azande method mentioned is that wherein two wooden boards, flattened and smoothed each on one side, are rubbed together. The boards mea-sure some five inches by two inches and may be decorated with bees-wax and seeds or beads on the outer surfaces. The few that have been collected come from the Mashi area of Barotseland.

Reel on String—*ngombo yalusango*

White terms this *ngombo yalusango*, the 'reel' used by the Luvale being a rattle (*insango*). The string, which measures some five or six feet in length, is hung from a convenient branch or beam and is kept taut by the diviner pinning the lower end to the ground with his foot. The rattle, through the centre of which a hole has been bored, is strung on the string and is thrown up it as the diviner puts his ques-tion. Should it stick and fail to fall then the reply is thereby given. This device is widely used, especially in witchfinding.

Instead of a rattle, a large nut-shell,[1] a gourd,[2] or a carved piece of wood resembling a mortar or cylinder in shape (Fig. 24(f)), may be used. One specimen in the Rhodes-Livingstone Museum is a large ball of beeswax moulded round a core (Fig. 24(d)). Beeswax is also often used on the wooden reels. As will be seen from the accompanying illustration (Fig. 24(g)), often the string does not pass straight through the reel but is looped round a nail or rod that is set across the hole in the reel. The diviner is, therefore, able surreptitiously to influence the result, merely by slightly increasing the tension on the string with his foot.

Magnetic Gourd (Fig. 24(c))

This was not noted in Barotseland but, in 1955, the writer found it in common use among the Masarwa, Bantu-ized Bushmen living in north-east Bechuanaland, a little to the south of the Protectorate and of the Caprivi Strip.

A section of gourd, saucer shaped and measuring some four to five inches in diameter by one to two inches in height, is laid mouth downward on a piece of animal hide, some nine to twelve inches square. The diviner grips the slippery greased back of the gourd in a peculiar fashion with thumb and last three fingers, across the knuckle of the index finger which is bent into the palm of the hand. If, on questioning, the gourd cannot be thus picked up but sticks, then the reply is deemed to have been given.

Kuntz (1932.133) mentions, in passing, divination by means of a magnetized cup but gives no further details.

REFLECTING

This is a method that must have been in use long before the arrival of the European and of glass mirrors. The principle is the same as that behind crystal gazing; the diviner peers into his crystal ball and sees therein the future, the *muloi* or the diagnosis.

Water

This reflecting device was most probably the earliest used, and it is possible that the soapstone bowls found at Zimbabwe were intended for this purpose.[3] Nowadays, a sophisticated public appears to

---

[1] By the Nganguela and Nyemba of Angola (Delachaux, 1946.47).
[2] By the Shona (Gelfand, 1956.115).
[3] I am indebted to Dr. J. D. Clark for this suggestion.

require of the diviner something more thrilling than gazing into a dish or pool of water. Doke (1931.272–273) records the use of this medium by a Lamba diviner, though in conjunction with a hand rattle. The diviner appears to have consulted the spirits through the rattle, but to have read the reply in a pot of water.

Actual Mirrors—siponi (Fig. 23(d) and (f))

Glass mirrors are now among the most popular of reflecting devices and may be used either unadorned or suitably decorated with beeswax, lucky beans or beads according to the taste of the diviner. One Totela specimen in the Rhodes-Livingstone Museum collections is set in the bottom of a basket. Mica is frequently used in magical practices but rarely for divining. The fragments of mica or glass set in the belly or chest of figurines may be so used, but there is no reliable evidence to confirm this.

The Shona *nganga* (Gelfand, 1956.115), when possessed, 'holds an ordinary mirror in his right hand into which he gazes whilst he pronounces the cause of illness. I am told that in years gone by a highly polished stone or crystal was used for this purpose.' No such use of polished stones or crystals has been noted in Barotseland.

Later in this chapter, witchfinding by means of *sikuyeti* charms is discussed. This method may also involve the use of a mirror, wherein the diviner sees the spirit or reflection of the *muloi*, in much the same way as a young girl in Europe is believed to see, through her mirror, the face of the man she will marry.

The following practice, observed in Mufulira a few years ago, combined both water and mirror methods. A doctor trained in Elizabethville used, for his divination, a bowl of water into which he peered via the reflection shown in a special mirror. The client threw coins into the bowl and the ripples reflected told of any hope of recovery. Should no ripples be reflected in the mirror, then there was no hope for the client in his malady and his money was returned.[1]

Magic Mirrors (Fig. 24(e))

These are not mirrors in the ordinary sense of the word, being oil gourds, bottles, skulls and similar containers all filled with medicine. They are, however, used in the same way as the reflecting mirrors described above.

---

[1] R. I. Cunningham; personal communication, 1958.

MENTAL DIVINATION

This is perhaps the most arbitrary of groupings; the criterion being the establishment of communication between the diviner and a familiar or ancestral spirit. This is achieved either through dreams, by going into a state of possession, or by employing a material symbol of the spirit or some similar object as the link with the spirit world.

According to Kuntz (1932.134–135; trans. by Turner, 1952. 54):

> The great diviner must once in his life, according to the Lozi, have killed a near relative, whom he turns into a ghost (*kanenga*) and through whom he enters into communication with the spirit world, and is able to speak to all the ghosts of the locality. He will demand of each its name and origin. Sometimes he will come upon a whole band of ghosts who have the same master; he will ask them the name of their master, then will ask each of them separately the way in which it met its death. When he has obtained full information he will return to the drums and begin to dance. After a time all grow silent. The diviner will relate what he learnt among the dead, and the names of the sorcerers, the masters of the ghosts he encountered. Then he will go among the groups of bystanders and examine each individual. When he reaches the author of the misfortunes he has been commissioned to dispel, he will see standing beside him the *silumba*, the spirit of the dead man he has killed.

As Kuntz noted, mental divination is only employed for the solution of serious problems, such as a series of deaths within a village, and a distinction is drawn between the 'great diviners' who use this method and the ordinary diviners who rely on the material devices described earlier in this chapter.

Figures and Figurines[1]

Some diviners make use in their practices of carved figures (Figs. 2, 3 and 4) and the familiars they symbolize. These familiars are the same as those employed by the sorcerer and witchdoctor.

Usually the diviner, in a state of possession, communicates with the spirit via the figure, whispering to it and listening to its equally secretive reply. The uninitiated onlookers are either unable to hear the latter or, if it is audible, unable to understand it. An Nkoya, on the Kabompo River, divined with the aid of a whistling figure, the

---

[1] The figurines in an *ngombo* divining basket function only as symbols within the confines of their basket and should not be confused with the figures and figurines discussed here.

noise being produced through a castor oil seed wedged in his own nostril.[1] A Kwandi diviner, in Senanga, was found practising a similar deception.

In contrast, a Lozi *kanameya* figure would whisper in the ear of its owner while he danced. This kind of figure is employed particularly in witchfinding and in the treatment of the bewitched. The most sinister would appear to be *kanenga*, *mwanankishi* and especially *likishi*. These indicate a *muloi*, either by whispering the guilty person's name in the ear of their master, or by moving through the village at night and pointing out his hut. This second practice is usually but a prelude to the destruction of the suspect.

Dancing

The diviner dances himself into a frenzy and into a state of possession ; he is then able to communicate directly with the spirits. Often this is merely an auxiliary or preliminary to another method, such as the use of figures. Its special value is that it helps to build up a suitable atmosphere at the consultation.

Radio (Fig. 26)

This is a sophisticated modern device observed only in Sesheke. A Luvale diviner set up a stick and very long string as mast and aerial, and proceeded to contact his spirits via a small 'radio', a hollowed out palm nut containing the nose and heart of a *jimina* rat. A number of charms were also used to protect the radio and the diviner from magical attack and the aerial from rain, while cloth tied round the stick helped to 'tune in' the voice of the spirit, which would otherwise be inaudible to the diviner. It is, of course, inaudible to everybody else anyway.

Dreams—kulola

Gelfand (1956.116) records the use of dreams by the Shona *nganga*, and Tonga diviners[2] are also known to employ this method. Very few references to divination through dreams were, however, recorded during the investigations, probably because no material device is employed. The diviner subsequently makes public the content of his dream, usually during a dance. The only equipment required, therefore, is a dancing outfit.

[1] R. I. Cunningham; personal communication, 1958.
[2] Field observation among the Valley Tonga, by the writer, 1957.

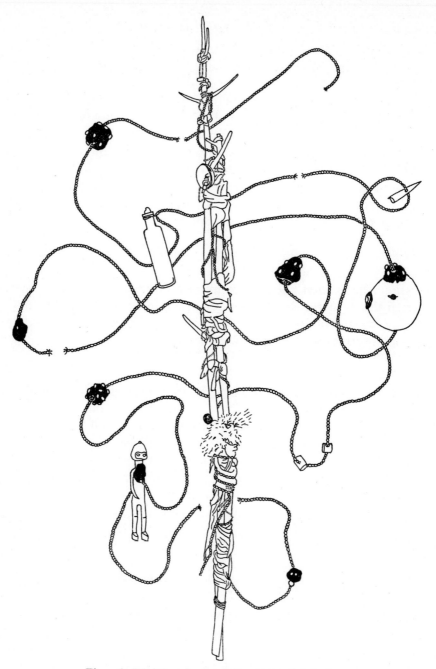

Fig. 26. Divining devices (vi); the 'radio' device

Direct Contact

It sometimes happens that a diviner establishes direct contact with the spirits or with his familiars by becoming possessed in front of his clients. He may dispense with these public preliminaries, preferring to work in private, and issue his decision in the form of a statement, as did the Totela diviner whose letter was quoted in Chapter II. A diviner would have to be very sure of himself, and at the same time command a great deal of respect, to divine in such a manner and expect to have his decision accepted.

DIVINATION THROUGH TREATMENT

In certain cases, mentioned already in Chapter III, the act of divination is inseparable from the curative treatment provided. For example, a *muba* doctor learns, by his patient's immediate reaction to treatment, whether he is in fact suffering from *muba* and whether a cure is likely. A typical reaction is for the patient to rise and dance with the doctor, or to be seized with a fit of trembling. Either act is involuntary. The treatment, it will be recalled, is not rational.

Certain anti-witchcraft practices are sometimes undertaken without knowing beforehand quite who the guilty person is. *Kaliloze* and *sikuyeti* doctoring are examples of these. The vengeance magic detects and then destroys the *muloi* responsible. It must be noted, however, that such 'divination' is not normally recognized by African laymen, who consider each of the doctors mentioned here as an *ng'aka* and not a *mulauli*.

ORDEAL

Divination by ordeal is widely employed throughout Africa and there are numerous references to and many detailed accounts of its use.[1] It has been argued that testing a suspect by ordeal is a legal rather than a divinatory device, for the suspect has already been pointed out or named by the witchfinder ; the ordeal merely tests his innocence or guilt. In many cases the suspect has indeed already been accused and is alone subjected to ordeal. In others, however, he is not, and the test is administered, either individually or simultaneously, to a group of suspects or even to the whole village. While the former could be considered a legal test, the latter is most certainly divination. Since we are concerned here with the description of

---

[1] For example, by Hoernlé (1937.240 ff.) and by Evans-Pritchard (1937).

methods employed in divination and witchfinding, regardless of their uses in other contexts, ordeals are included.

The ordeal test may be applied not only in cases of witchcraft but also in cases of theft and of other crimes. Melland (1923.223) notes, however, that poison (*mwavi*) is used by the Kaonde only in witchcraft cases.

Poison—mwafi (LUYANA); mwazi (LUNDA-LUVALE)

This is the most widely used form of ordeal. Although no cases were reported during the Barotse investigations, one occurred in Kalabo in 1953. It is administered either to human suspects or to their representatives, such as chickens, the most expendable form of native livestock.

Humans. A rather astringent emetic is prepared and administered to each suspect. The innocent will vomit, not necessarily immediately; the guilty will not and will, therefore, it is believed, die of poison. This fear and the sharp stomach pains caused by the brew prey on his mind as he sits, uneasily and in silence, with his fellow suspects.[1] His nerve eventually gives way and he confesses. All need to vomit and wash out their stomachs with water. In cases of witchcraft where, it may be assumed, there is no real miscreant, the 'guilty' will himself only realize his offence as he watches his neighbours thankfully succumb to the emetic. Any feelings of hostility he may have had towards the victim are magnified as he searches his conscience, and crystallize into a feeling of guilt. He may then be expected to confess to his imagined crime. One doctor in the Copperbelt introduced a variation. Vomiting was a sign of guilt; inability to vomit a sign of innocence.

In the Copperbelt and Northern Province, the emetic is usually an infusion of the bark or root of *Erythrophloeum guineense* : '(These) are very poisonous, producing a severe diarrhoea and vomiting and have a digitalis-like action on the heart. The tree contains a mixture of alkaloids, the major one being cassaine.' (Fanshawe and Hough, 1960.8.) An infusion of the inner bark of *Crossopteryx febrifuga* was also, at one time, used by the Chewa : 'The bark contains a poisonous alkaloid, rhynchophylline, producing a lowering of the blood pressure and a glycoside, B-quinorine.' (ibid. 5.)

---

[1] 'Vomiting is a physiological mechanism. It is a defense reaction that tends to liberate the organism of noxious substances, but it is one that has a strong nervous and emotional element.' (Sigerist, 1951.186.)

White and Melland (1923.222–223) note the use of this test for the LUNDA-LUVALE and the Kaonde respectively. The latter notes that the emetic is mixed with beer.

In Barotseland, the use of the poison ordeal was banned by Lewanika in 1891. According to Gluckman's (1955.97–98) informants, it was used prior to that date to test sorcerers:

the alleged sorcerer was first isolated from a number of suspects by a diviner and then taken to the *kuta*. On a special mound near Lealui, he was seated on a platform over a fire and given *mwafi* (a plant containing strychnine) to drink. If the *mwafi* stupefied him so that he fell into the fire, he was guilty and was killed; if he vomited the *mwafi* he was innocent. (Coillard and other pioneers of the Paris Evangelical Mission, which entered Loziland in 1884, reported that many people were killed thus.)

The test could also be used in secret: 'since sorcery mainly harms their own kin, when members of an (extended) family suspect one of themselves to be a sorcerer, they will secretly give him *mwafi* in his beer. If he vomits it and shows he is innocent, they commiserate with him on the bad beer; if he dies, they bury him and no one outside the family knows.'

In late 1958, in Solwezi district, North-Western Province, a witchdoctor accused a man of being a *muloi*. On denying this the accused was compelled to eat 'an exceedingly noxious paste substance' to prove his innocence. The paste was on a charmed spoon which 'if he had lied would have killed him'.

Chickens. White describes this form of ordeal as follows (vomiting is a sign of innocence, death a sign of guilt):

The test is administered by an infusion of *mwazi*, a vegetable substance obtained from the root of a tree. It is administered to the fowl by a funnel. In some cases, where several people mutually suspect each other of causing death or calamity, all may produce fowls and apply the test. In other cases, where one person is suspected, the accusers may buy fowls from him and administer the test in private. If the fowl dies they will return and accuse him by presenting him with the dead fowl or a part of it, while if the fowl survives its owner will have it returned to him as proof of the fact that he has been the victim of wrong suspicions.

When the fowl, by vomiting or dying, has provided an answer, this is checked by the same question, in negative form, being posed and a second fowl given the poison.

White also notes the application of this test to decide the efficacy of malignant charms ; in the case he gives as an example, the test is of a *kaliloze* gun.

With regard to the Kaonde preliminary test (Melland, 1923. 223), made also among the Ila (Smith and Dale, 1920.II.356–357), wherein, before the ordeal is administered to any suspects, *mwavi* is given to a fowl to find whether the misfortune was in fact due to witchcraft, White considers, 'among the Lunda and Lwena the *mwazi* test appears to require the use of fowls in relation to some specific person or object.'

Boiling Water

This is a traditional ordeal in Barotseland and, until Lewanika abolished the practice, was used to test not only *baloi* but also thieves. Arnot (1889.66, 92, and 94) records that such tests were of almost daily occurrence, and describes one which he observed :

A small company gathered in front of my hut, and began an animated discussion, which grew hotter and hotter, and shortly a large fire was kindled, and a pot of water set on it. I was told that this was a trial for witchcraft, and that the two persons charged had to wash their hands in the water, and if, after twenty-four hours, the skin came off, the victims were to be burned alive. First one, then the other, dipped his hands in the fiercely-boiling water, lifting some up and pouring it over the wrist. Twenty-four hours told its tale, and I saw the poor fellows marched off to be burned before a howling cursing crowd.

Elsewhere, he notes the cool behaviour of the suspects and later recounts an interesting instance of a man proving his innocence by this means :

I saw him twice dip his hands into boiling water, allowing the water to run over his wrists as he lifted his hands out, and yet today his skin seems quite natural. The only cause for this I can think of is that he is nearly a century old, and his hands are as tough as tough can be. This was flourished before me as a great victory, achieved under my very eyes, in favour of the boiling pot trials. The advocates for this particular piece of barbarism declare that if the hands of an infant who knew nothing of witchcraft were placed in boiling water, not a particle of skin would come off.

The Kaonde (Melland, 1923.229) employ the boiling water test (*mwavi wa wombwe*) only for minor matters, such as adultery or theft, but never for serious crimes such as witchcraft. Again there is a de-

Divining with a basket

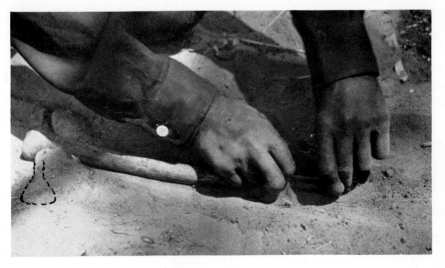

Divining with an axe

lay of twenty-four hours before the hands of the accused are in-
spected.

Innumerable examples of the use of the boiling water test by different tribes could be given, for it is to be found throughout much of
south and south-central Africa.

Gluckman's (1955.98–99) informants stated that a suspected thief
was required to take a stone out of boiling water. Hoernlé (1937.
240) records exactly the same test for thieves among the South-
Eastern Bantu.

Hot Iron

In Barotseland another form of ordeal, now forbidden, was used
to test suspected thieves. These were compelled 'to lick at hot iron.
. . . Fat was then rubbed on the . . . skin, and if a blister formed, the
accused was guilty.' (Gluckman, 1955.98–99.) The Shona (Gelfand,
1956.62) formerly used this test, as did also the South-Eastern
Bantu (Hoernlé, 1937.250).

Miscellaneous

The Luvale diviner who employed the 'radio' device in Sesheke
practised a second method of witchfinding ; this also he had learned in
the Congo. The suspect was balanced rather precariously on a stone,
and a genet skin wrapped round his neck. A sharp tug at the skin
would either unbalance him, thereby demonstrating his innocence,
or leave him unmoved, thus proclaiming his guilt. One or two other
diviners in Sesheke and its environs also used this method.

Where murder by witchcraft is suspected, the corpse itself may be
used to find the witch responsible. The villagers or suspects are
gathered in a circle and the corpse, laid in a stretcher suspended from
a pole, is carried round by two men. As they move the stretcher
swings. The person whom it touches is believed to be the witch.[1]

In 1953, at Kalabo, a Lozi witchfinder was arrested. He had made
each suspect in turn stand on a rough stone, the size of a man's head.
The stone was partially sunk in the ground to make it firm, and the
upper surface was flat. Should a man begin to tremble whilst on the
stone this would indicate that he was possessed by an evil spirit (*?mu-
loi*). The balanced suspect was required to hold a small charmed clay
pot in the left hand and a medicated horn in the right. The diviner
danced round him during the test.

[1] Observed in Mankoya, about 1935, by G. C. R. Clay; personal communication, 1961.

In 1957, in Mankoya, an ex-soldier was found practising a 'boiling bottle' test. He would blow a whistle,

> and shout 'Fall in' in English, whereupon the villagers would form a line. He would then go down the line and invite the people to shake a bottle; if it foamed they were witches or had some charms; if it did not they were clear. . . . He had two identical bottles, one full of water, the other of eardrops; and . . . one bottle had a chip off the cork so that feeling in his pocket he could select the appropriate one for each person.[1]

In one case record there is mention of divining with snuff. No further details were available, but it was probably administered to the patient or suspect in much the same way as the Shona (Gelfand, 1956.173) *nganga* gives a powder made from the *kapende* tree. If the patient (accused) sneezes, he will recover (is innocent); if he does not, he will die (is guilty).

Finally, where a diviner seeks out cannibals and necrophagers he does it with his nose, for they have on their fingers the smell of the human flesh they have handled. This smell is only perceptible by witchfinders and by similar experts who, to emphasize their peculiar powers, frequently sniff vigorously when in the company of other people.

This list of divining devices, employed in Barotseland and in neighbouring areas, is by no means exhaustive. The number of devices noted, for which no details of usage were available, serves to emphasize this. The list does, however, indicate something of the range of divining techniques and the way in which the diviner works.

Most of the devices here described depend, for their efficacy, not on any intrinsic power of their own but, as Turner (1961.73) explains, on powers vested in the diviner. The device merely serves as a means of giving expression to the replies to his questions.

Almost all divining methods are open to manipulation on the part of the diviner. Yet, whether he truly believes in his own powers, whether, consciously or unconsciously, he influences the replies of his device is, in a sense, immaterial. The main thing is that he has the confidence of his audience and that they have faith in his abilities. This is where he is of value to society. He provides understandable causes of misfortune, causes against which the services of the *ng'aka* may be enlisted. In so doing he confirms the value of going on living

---

[1] District Commissioner, Mankoya; personal communication, 1957.

despite adversities. Where the diviner indicates a witch, he is providing an acceptable scapegoat on whom the community may vent its pent-up feelings. In so doing he is, of course, guilty of an offence under the Witchcraft Ordinance. As White (1961.65) points out, 'It is an ironical feature of the cases prosecuted under the Witchcraft Ordinance that diviners are the people most commonly charged with naming a witch although they are generally merely the mouthpiece of corporate hostility towards the suspected witch.'

CHAPTER V

THE *SITONDO*

To the subsistence cultivators of southern Africa, the weather is of considerable and continued importance. It can make or mar the crops, cause famine and hardship, or fill the granaries to overflowing. It is understandable, therefore, that intense interest should be shown in its behaviour.

The LUNDA-LUVALE (McCulloch, 1951.73) believe that only the Supreme God, Nzambi, controls the weather and can give or withhold rain, and that he must be approached through the ancestral spirits. If at planting times the rains are late, a special ceremony (*musolu*) is held and prayers made to him. Similar beliefs are held by most central African peoples. The Kaonde consider rain as a gift from Lesa, their Supreme God, who also controls the thunder and lightning. Melland (1923.154–155) specifically observes, 'There are no "rain makers" among the Kaonde : rainmaking is not an accomplishment of doctor or chief.' If the rains are late, a ceremony similar to *musolu*, except that the ancestral spirits are ignored, is held and prayers offered to Lesa. Among the Ila (Smith and Dale, 1920.II. 220) too, rain and the weather generally are believed to be controlled by Lesa. While, in a storm, men pray or plead that they may not be harmed, this is a spontaneous action by individuals; there are no specialists or professionals who act on behalf of clients or neighbours. Pointing a pestle at brilliant rainbows to prevent rain from falling may also be practised by any individual. The rain cults of the Plateau and Valley Tonga (Colson, 1948 and 1960) and the annual ritual at rain shrines are also attempts to obtain the sympathy of Lesa though, as among the LUNDA-LUVALE, spiritual intermediaries (*basungu*) have to be employed.

Among these tribes then the weather is believed to be controlled by the Supreme God, and its behaviour is a matter of concern not just for the individual but for the community as a whole. Any action is on a communal basis and takes the form of prayers and invocations to the God. There is no claim, however, that any control is thereby exercised over the weather, although the keeper of the shrine may have some reputation as a rainmaker.

THE *SITONDO*

Arnot (1889.78) noted in 1883:

an old but waning belief that a chief is a demi-god, and in heavy thunder-storms the Barotse flock to the chief's yard for protection from the lightning . . . (or) fall on their knees before the chief, entreating him to open the water pots of heaven and send rain upon their gardens. But last year the chief (Lewanika) acknowledged to me that he knew he was unable to do so.

Since Lozi royals were believed to be descended from Nyambe, the Supreme God (Turner, 1952.49), it may be supposed that the chief was believed to be able either to control the weather himself or to intercede with Nyambe on behalf of his subjects.

Nowadays, in Barotseland, the problem is treated differently. There is no organized rain cult and the problem is left in the hands of individual specialist raindoctors (*sitondo*, pl. *basitondo*), who act on behalf of their villages, their neighbours and their clients. This is not to say that there is less interest in the weather and the rain. The weather is of especial importance to the inhabitants of the Barotse plain, for it not only affects the planting and growth of their crops but also the existence of the gardens themselves. If the floods come out of season, as happened in 1957 and 1958, these are swept away. Further, the floods affect the very dwellings of the villagers, causing them to move to the safety of the higher ground at the fringe of the plain for part of the year.

A *sitondo*, or *ng'aka wa pula* as he is often called, is required to control both lightning and rain, and should be able not only to ward off an undesired storm but also to direct either of these two elements to a particular place. Thus, in theory, he should be able to call rain to the gardens of his own village and, at the same time, deprive the gardens of another. He should be able to ward off lightning strikes from his own territory and, if desired, direct them against some other village or person. Just as the *ng'aka ya baloi* (doctor of witches), through his ability to control dangerous elements, is feared as a possible sorcerer so, for the same reason, is the raindoctor feared.

The name, *sitondo*, is also given to those men who are able to control wild animals. Such doctors are believed not only to direct the activities of, but even to assume the shape of the type of beast they control. Lions, crocodiles and hyenas are especially associated with this practice, and their masters are termed *ng'aka wa litau* (doctor of lions), *ng'aka wa likwena* (doctor of crocodiles) and *ng'aka wa sitongwani* (doctor of hyenas) respectively. These *sitondo* are, like the *ng'aka wa pula*, considered to practise sorcery, as well as to protect the community from the beasts they control and to cure any wounds they may cause. As Kuntz (1932.128) notes, with reference to the *ng'aka wa litau* (*l'homme-lion*), wounds inflicted on a beast that a *sitondo* temporarily inhabits will be evident on that *sitondo* when he returns to human form.

Since we are here considering only those doctors who are concerned with rain and weather control, the term *sitondo* is used, throughout the remainder of this chapter, as a synonym for *ng'aka wa pula*.

Gelfand (1956.24), discussing rainmaking in Mashonaland, where it is the concern of the *mhondoro* (tribal spirit), deplores the use of the term 'raindoctor' and prefers to use 'rainmaker'. The concern of a doctor (*nganga*), he considers, 'is the health of individuals, or of a small community, whereas rain is a matter that is vital to the whole tribe.' For the LUYANA and their neighbours, however, this is not the case, and rain control is very much the concern of the individual. 'Raindoctor' is, therefore, the appropriate term to use. This is also more in keeping with Barotse ideas, for *ng'aka wa pula*, when translated literally, means 'a doctor of rain'. The Shona also differentiate between rainmaking and the control of thunder and lightning.[1] The Barotse do not; the *ng'aka wa pula* deals with both.

It might be argued from the use of the term, *ng'aka wa pula*, that the raindoctor is but a specialist *ng'aka* and should be included in Chapter III. Informants agree, however, that raindoctoring is a distinctly separate practice and should be described accordingly in a chapter of its own. The confusion as to whether or not a *sitondo* is an *ng'aka* arises from the fact that most, if not all *sitondo* are able to treat injuries caused by lightning. By so doing they become herbal doctors and, therefore, *ng'aka* proper. Should they restrict their activities to rain and lightning direction, they are merely *sitondo*.

A contributory factor to the confusion lies in the frequent application of the name, *sitondo*, to all *ng'aka* irrespective of their ability to control the weather. Where a *sitondo* uses his powers to harm others he is, of course, entering the field of sorcery. The same applies when he uses lightning as an agent for the transmission of *siposo*. This is believed to be a very common practice, though it must be pointed out that many of the sorcerers and witchdoctors using lightning *siposo*

---

[1] Gelfand (1956.106) considers the latter a doctor.

are not raindoctors.[1] Their powers are limited to this one field. Admittedly, they may often be called *sitondo* but this is because, on cloudy days or during rain, it is unwise to refer to a raindoctor by his proper name ; to do so would dry up the rain and disperse the clouds. Since *ng'aka* do not usually advertise their limitations, their neighbours are often in doubt as to whether they are in fact raindoctors as well. To be on the safe side they address them as *sitondo*.

The equipment of the raindoctor is quite simple. It consists usually of two or three items, of which the most important is the charm that actually controls the weather. This may be either a flyswitch (*muhata*) (Figs. 8, 9 and 10), a carved stick, a horn (*mushengo*) filled with medicine (Figs. 11 and 12), or python skin belts or armbands (*muulu*) (Fig. 18). In all cases the charms have been previously medicated to give them the required powers. Other charms of a similar nature, which are intended to protect the doctor in his battles with the elements, are also employed.

When a storm blows up and lesser mortals cower under shelter, the doctor walks out into the open, singing and shouting to the oncoming clouds ; the content of his incantations is, it would seem, a set formula. He faces the bad weather and waves his charm at the clouds. If he is using a flyswitch, he usually makes gestures of flicking away the storm. The performance may be carried on for quite a long time, until the clouds begin to disperse.

The 'shepherd of heaven' of the South-Eastern Bantu[2] and the thunder and lightning doctor of the Shona (Gelfand, 1956.106–107) carry out similar performances and the latter, like the *sitondo* of Barotseland, also treats burns and injuries caused by lightning.

Both the South-Eastern Bantu tribes and the Shona have a belief in a 'bird of heaven' which comes down with the lightning and lays its eggs where the lightning strikes. These 'eggs' are dug up by the doctor, for they are believed to possess valuable magical properties, which can be incorporated in rain or lightning charms or in medicines for burns. A similar belief is held in Barotseland.

Where protection against lightning is required for a house, a medicated horn may be hung in the doorway. Where rain is desired, the doctor may either go through a set ritual, perhaps in the village or in

---

[1] Gelfand (1956.106) also distinguishes between the thunder and lightning doctor and the *chikwambo nganga*, who is believed to use lightning as a weapon.

[2] Hoernlé (1937.234). These doctors guard against 'lightning, hail and storm and the greatest of them (provide) rain under the direction of the chief'.

the gardens, or he may place a charm, such as a horn or gourd, out in the open to induce the rain to fall.

Raindoctoring and weather control are only practised by men. The charms and training necessary are obtained from practising raindoctors in return for money or payment in kind or through inheritance. Any layman interested in the practice can choose a *sitondo* and ask for charms. These are of two kinds—defensive, to drive away the lightning or to call up rain ; and offensive, to enable the user to send lightning against or to withhold rain from others. For a first payment, the doctor supplies his apprentice with defensive charms and teaches him their use. If the latter wishes to become a full doctor, he must return and purchase a second set of, this time, offensive charms. The purchase price of these charms would not appear to be very great ; ten shillings was one price mentioned.

Defensive and offensive charms are similar in appearance, and often it is not possible to distinguish between the full doctor and the apprentice. Unless, however, a man possesses the latter, he is not a *sitondo*, merely a client or apprentice. It is understandable that many headmen consult raindoctors and purchase defensive charms to protect their villages. These are placed on the peak of the headman's house or in a similarly prominent position. Their possession does not mean, however, that the owner is a *sitondo*. In fact, it is reasonable to conclude that a full *sitondo*, by reason of his supposed power for evil as well as for good, would not normally prove a popular headman.

Most of the cases of raindoctoring recorded come from LUYANA and ASSIMILATED LUYANA tribes. Only two were from LUNDA-LUVALE tribes and both were Mbunda, probably as a result of LUYANA influence. The Lozi[1] view that the Old Mbunda and the Mashi are great rainmakers was not borne out by the investigations of 1956 and 1957.

To conclude, *sitondo* are raindoctors who practise alone and without any form of organization. They are reputed to possess powers for both good and ill, and usually not only attempt to manipulate the weather, but also treat any burns or wounds caused by lightning. Although their work is of considerable importance and interest in everyday life, they have not the opportunities for fame and prestige that the *ng'aka*, especially the witchdoctor, has. As a result they are only locally of social and political importance.

[1] Gluckman (1941. Chart 8); see also Chapter VII below.

CHAPTER VI

THE TWELVE SOCIETY

In 1957, the existence of a rather unusual society was noted in Mongu district. This society, the Twelve Society, specialized in the treatment and cure of *bindele*, one of the modern LUNDA-LUVALE *mahamba* noted by White (1949) and discussed earlier in Chapter III. It will be recalled that while *mahamba* are traditionally ailments resulting from possession by ancestral spirits, the modern version are caused by possession by other spirits and may be considered to reflect a tension between the society of the victim and that of the group represented by the spirit. Sufferers from *bindele*, which is the Luvale word for 'European',[1] are believed to be possessed by the spirit of an European. This is by no means unusual for, as McCulloch (1951. 78) notes, 'Common sources of origin (of the new *mahamba*) are Europeans and travellers from the Songo and Mbande areas west of the Luchazi area in Angola,' and she quotes examples, such as *cimbandu*, which requires a treatment involving dressing and eating as an European, and *ndeke* (aeroplane), which occurs in areas where aeroplanes are frequently seen.

Mahamba ailments are normally treated by individual *ng'aka* and the patient, once cured, is free to go his way. If he so wishes, he may be initiated as a doctor of the ailment and may then leave to practise on his own. The Twelve Society shows an unusual change in this pattern, and a description[2] of its history and activities will, it is felt, be of interest.

The Twelve Society was founded in 1944 by Rice Kamanga, a trader, now known as Chana I. Very little is known of Kamanga's early life other than that, as a small boy, he accompanied his father when he moved from Angola to Northern Rhodesia. From 1928 to 1934, he attended a Seventh Day Adventist School in Kalabo district and, a year or so later, went to work in Southern Rhodesia. So far his career was typical of that of many youths of the territory. Whether he ever became a member of the Seventh Day Adventist Church is

---

[1] The Lozi term for both European and *bindele* is *mukua*.

[2] I am indebted to I. H. Wethey for information on the Twelve Society and, in this chapter, have drawn very heavily on his report (Mongu district files, 1957).

unknown; so many apparent converts at mission schools, whatever their denomination, are interested in the material rather than the spiritual benefits that can be derived. Neither is anything known of Kamanga's life or activities in Southern Rhodesia, and he does not come to public notice until 1944, when it would appear that he became mentally ill and ran off into the bush.

In due course Kamanga, apparently cured, returned to his village and related his experiences. He claimed that, during his wanderings, he had been visited by a spirit which had informed him that he was suffering from *bindele* and had not only explained how he might be cured, but had also commanded him to become a doctor specializing in the treatment of this ailment. Doubtless, his experiences and new-found knowledge were frequently discussed and, as was to be expected, a number of unfortunates soon discovered that they were victims of the new malady and accordingly put themselves in Kamanga's hands.

The spirit had also told Kamanga, or Chana as he is now better known, to found a new church or society and to name it the Twelve Society, after the first twelve patients that he cured. This he duly did and installed these twelve as doctors of *bindele*. All of them, however, are subordinate to himself and, with two exceptions, their doctoring is confined to acting as agents or receptionists, whose prime duties are to interview potential clients and to bring them to Chana for treatment. It would seem that even the diagnosis is made by the latter. After diagnosis, the subordinate doctor is responsible for ensuring that the patient follows the course of treatment prescribed.

The two exceptions are, firstly, Chamba who, during the time that Chana was away serving a prison sentence, acted as leader of the society, and secondly, Chimbweta, otherwise known as Chana II, who is responsible to Chana I for the organization of the society in Senanga district. Chana is directly responsible for its organization in the three northern districts of Kalabo, Mankoya and Mongu. The last-named contains his headquarters and church. So rapid has been the growth of the society, that the church he built in his village in the early days soon proved too small and, in 1952, he built a second and larger one.

There is a definite and recognized order of seniority among the Twelve, though it would seem that this has no relation to relative importance. Chana II is only number four on the list while Chamba, the master's understudy, is the most junior of all. The actual list reads:

1. Mingochi	7. Mucima
2. Makai	8. Kamboi Mbangu
3. Kahuma	9. Lukuba
4. Chimbweta (Chana II)	10. Dickson Chibinda
5. Tapalo	11. Kaliamba
6. Nyangambo (a woman)	12. Chamba

It is to be noted that there is only one female.[1]

Chana's treatment consists of interviewing the patient outside the gate of his *pazo*,[2] and testing whether or not he has the disease by ringing bells and talking to him, whereupon the sick man, if he is afflicted with *bindele*, should begin trembling and shouting. That night there is further examination accompanied by much singing and drumming, when the patient goes into a frenzy and performs a strange dance whilst sitting on a little stool. His finale is to fall over a small jar of chalk (*pepa*), which is placed in front of him on another stool, and this is taken as definite proof that he has *bindele* disease.

After remaining the night in Chana's village, both the patient and the subordinate doctor go to the former's village, where a small circular windbreak (*hupa*) of grass is built. In this the patient must now live until he is cured, a lengthy process that may take from one to five months. During this time he must collect such roots and leaves as he is required to do by the possessing spirit, pound them up in a wooden trough specially carved for the purpose, and bathe himself once, twice or even thrice daily or as urged by his tormentor. He must also drink some of the mixture.

The whole emphasis of the treatment is on cleanliness. The patient must be supplied with clean blankets and, if female, clean white clothes. Logically, he or she must be fed on European food, or rather the type of food that is favoured by urban Africans—tea, bread and the like. The patient's relatives and wife are responsible for feeding him during this period. A different kind of cleansing is that whereby the spirit demands that the patient surrenders any witchcraft charms he may possess.

During this period the subordinate doctor remains nearby, though he never enters the shelter. Once the patient is cured, he is instructed by his spirit to destroy the windbreak. Both doctor and patient there-

[1] Whereas White (1949) notes that women are overwhelmingly the main victims of the modern *mahamba*.

[2] An enclosed courtyard containing a small hut and the three trees mentioned below.

upon return to report to Chana, who waits till a Saturday and then takes his patient into the church in order to check whether the cure is genuine. Again Chana's supremacy is emphasized by the fact that he alone may take a patient into the church.

In church,[1] Chana's doctors assemble and sit along the left and right walls in order of seniority. Number 2 and Number 3 share the bay with Chana. The patient stands at the top of the cross (*mbwilinga*) and Chana stands in front of the bay. Chana then talks to the patient, who starts shaking and eventually falls over the cross holding himself off the ground with his hands. After Chana has finished talking to him, he tells the patient to rise and come to the *Malimalima*[2] which is suspended from the roof in the centre of the church. Sometimes the spirits will hold the patient down and then Chana will go to him, walking around the patient mumbling and stamping his right foot on the ground, until the patient rises.

The patient then goes to the *Malimalima* and faces Chana, who asks him finally whether he is cured of *bindele* disease. The patient will again start to shake and will fall forward and grab one of the five metal discs on the cross-bar of the *Malimalima*. These discs are round, made of pieces of flat iron and have numerous holes stamped through them. The one on the right is black and the other four are red. If the patient grabs one of the red discs it is a sign that he is cured and then he is invited to take a chair next to the other doctors. Then follows a sing-song. The songs are completely harmless, like 'my mother is coming and we must all be glad'. After the sing-song Chana addresses the gathering. Members of the public are allowed in and the church is normally full. His speech is, according to my information, stereotyped and has a good theme. He tells the people to eat good and better food, keep their houses and villages clean, look after their children, take daily baths, etc. The patient and Chana then leave the church and then comes the real test, whether the patient is cured or not.

The patient is now taken into Chana's *pazo* for the test. This is a most respected enclosure and could perhaps be termed the 'holy of holies'.

The patient enters and faces the centre of three trees. This tree has a needle[3] in its trunk. Chana stands behind him and again talks to him, and asks him whether he is sure that he is cured. The patient again starts shaking and will fall forward and grab the trunk of the centre tree with both hands. This is then the final sign that he is cured and he leaves the *pazo*.

---

[1] Unfortunately, it has not been possible to trace the plan of the church that accompanied this report.

[2] *Malimalima* normally means 'spinning top' but it is not clear whether it is used in this sense here.

[3] Whether this is another use of the needle charm described in Chapter III is not clear.

Chana then tells him what he has to pay. Payment is normally in the form of livestock; a cow, a few pigs or goats, but frequently, a fairly substantial sum of money has to be paid. He must also bring a beast to slaughter for the feast that night.

The beast is slaughtered and the feast is on and lasts the whole night with drumming and singing. The patient is placed on a mound of sand during this final ceremony and not on the stool.

The next day the patient is installed as a doctor and he goes with his doctor to his village, where they build a *pazo* for him, on the same pattern as Chana's *pazo*. *Pepa* (chalk) is found for him by his doctor, but his bells he must buy himself. He is now entitled to receive patients and take them to Chana.

The *pazo* of the ordinary doctor is only used to keep his *pepa* and bells in. No patient is ever taken into it.

Patients are always cured. There are no failures.

The extent of Chana's borrowings from the Seventh Day Adventists is obvious. The cross, the spirit, the Twelve Apostles, the church and the restriction of its use to Saturdays are all ideas of which the roots in Chana's mind must stretch back to his schooldays. Their employment shows little other than ingenuity and the ability to adapt them to the new cult. Chana's ability must not, however, be too strongly decried. He was fortunate in covering his society with an aura of European respectability, by using such practices and methods as would strike sympathetic chords in the minds of Christians and those educated at mission schools. At the same time, his skilful development of the society is in many ways to be admired. Unlike other ordinary African doctors, he keeps the patient as the centre of attraction all the time and thereby renders him very amenable to treatment. Again, instead of allowing his cured patients to break away and set up as independent *bindele* doctors, he keeps them under control, thus increasing the prestige and power of his own organization and also avoiding the emergence of rivals. To strengthen his control of the organization, or rather of its members, he has reserved certain important powers for himself and, at the same time, established a hierarchy among his immediate subordinates, thereby preventing them from uniting against him. Perhaps to this may be attributed the apparently illogical employment of the most junior 'apostle' as his understudy. Chamba would be the least likely usurper of his subordinates.

By the emphasis on the cleansing of the patient's witchcraft propensities, the Twelve Society has no doubt obtained much popular support. No patient, having demonstrated that he had been a sorcerer, would be able to return to his practice; similarly, a diviner or witchdoctor who cast away his equipment in obedience to the command of the *bindele* spirit would be unlikely to have the courage to return to his practice. Whether, as Wethey suggests, Chana considered that he was thereby obtaining the approval of the authorities, is a matter for conjecture.

A considerable number of *bindele* patients appears to have possessed witchcraft charms, for a large heap had accumulated near the church. When removed in 1957, by the District Commissioner, they filled six large sacks. While this collection contained a considerable quantity of unidentifiable material, such as medicated horns, that could have been innocuous, there was a fairly high proportion of items that were definitely similar to objects used in witchdoctoring and divining. This contrasts with Richards' (1935.45) experience on examining a similar heap of *mucapi* witchcraft objects. She found that of the 135 horns and charms in the heap, only 10 were possibly or definitely suspicious. The remainder were definitely harmless.

To suggest that Chana's motives in starting his society were purely monetary, in order to finance his stores, is rather too simple a solution. Admittedly, the charge for treatment is high, but it is not much higher than that for the treatment of less popular, more mundane ailments. It is also rather unlikely that the whole sequence of events, from the original disappearance into the bush to the establishment and naming of the society, were planned beforehand. A more reasonable explanation is that Chana did actually believe that he was visited by a spirit. When he came back to his village, he may or may not have been planning to set up as a *bindele* doctor but when, as is common practice, people came to him complaining of the same troubles and asking his help, no doubt he decided to do so. As the 'disease' became more and more popular so did the scope for his ambitions increase. Since the treatment took a fairly long time, he had time to think about the future and to plan accordingly. His rewards are also not merely monetary. He has built up a following, the members of which are dependent on him and look to him as their leader while, outside the society, his importance is recognized and socially, politically, as well as economically, his standing is much improved.

CHAPTER VII

THE CASE RECORDS

Introduction

The material for this analysis was collected in January, 1958,[1] from records of 1,212 cases heard by district officers sitting as magistrates in Class II and Class III subordinate courts at Kalabo, Mongu, Senanga and Sesheke during the period October 1956 to January 1958. In these four districts 175, 702, 264 and 71 cases were heard respectively. All, with the exception of those involving charges of necrophagy, were brought under the Witchcraft Ordinance. Twenty-six cases of suicide and one of attempted suicide relevant to this study are also included.

Since, towards the end of 1957, only fifteen cases had then been heard at Mankoya, it was decided that the records there would not be examined. The sudden and unexpected influx of cases, some fifty or sixty, that occurred in this district towards the end of the following year, came too late for inclusion in this analysis.

Cases heard in the High Court or by the Resident Magistrate are also not included.

The Witchcraft Ordinance[2] defines witchcraft as, 'including the throwing of bones, the use of charms and any other means, process or device, adopted in the practice of witchcraft or sorcery.' Provided that a practice can be shown to be witchcraft, no further definition is required. This has made the task of sorting difficult, and records have often had to be discarded because they fail to give sufficient information for the practice to which they refer to be identified. For example, 89 records of divining practices give no indication of the device employed. Because of this omission much of their value is lost. Other records state even less and have, therefore, had to be discarded completely.

Often, in a record, only those practices which were of prime importance to the case were noted. For example, a man who was both a *kaliloze* gunman and also a herbal doctor is likely to have been de-

[1] By Mr. P. J. A. Rigby. I have also drawn upon notes made during my own visits to Barotseland in 1957.
[2] Quoted in full in the Appendix.

139

scribed only as the former. The frequency with which the same individual carried on different practices, as noted in many fuller reports, makes one suspect the great extent of such plurality.

Finally, those records of cases of consulting, employing or protecting a witchdoctor[1] have been discarded. These total 189. It is most probable that many of the other records discarded, because of their lack of identifying data, are also of consulting, employing or carrying out the directions of a witchdoctor. Since the offenders were charged, as were many 'witchdoctors', with the possession of charms it is most difficult to separate these cases. Further, a number of cases relate to matters that are not truly witchcraft; for example, the control of crocodiles at a cattle crossing by means of a charmed paddle, the possession of a charm as a defence against snakes. Charms such as the latter may, as has been shown, be obtained from knowledgeable laymen without recourse to witchdoctors.

Cases of needle wearing have not been discarded, because of the connection of this practice with the use of *siposo* and of *kaliloze* guns. Again, reporting is uneven and reflects the gradual decline of interest in the practice, on the part of the authorities, and the corresponding decline in importance of needles, from being regarded as tallies of murders, to mere charms against illness.

Prosecutions

District officers are usually reluctant to bring reputed witchdoctors to court unless there is a very strong case against them and every likelihood that their guilt will be proved. For a prosecution to be unsuccessful is tantamount to giving the accused official sanction for his work, an impression to be avoided. Witnesses are frequently unreliable, being easily frightened by the supposed magical power of the accused, and so magistrates usually prefer material evidence of guilt, in the form of the equipment of the practitioner, on which to base their decisions. All that is then necessary is to prove that the equipment is associated with witchcraft, and to establish ownership. A considerable number of accusations and complaints must, therefore, never result in prosecution, either because the district officer, investigating in his capacity of policeman, considers that they are malicious, or that the evidence is too weak, or the witnesses too unreliable, to produce a conviction. One may conclude, firstly, that numerous as the prosecutions have been, by no means all the suspected diviners,

[1] This term was freely used for almost all kinds of offenders.

doctors and sorcerers have been gathered in, and that any attempt to produce a ratio for the Protectorate of Number of Magicians : Total Population from these figures would err considerably ; secondly, and more important, that the fact that many magicians escaped scatheless is fully appreciated by the inhabitants of the Protectorate. No doubt, in so doing, their reputation for invulnerability was greatly enhanced.

The District Commissioner, Kalabo,[1] noted, for example, 'About 150 other persons were brought in for investigation and were released without being tried either because it was not considered expedient to prosecute or because there was insufficient evidence.' And, 'It is, after all, quite easy to destroy or conceal a *kaliloze* gun. It was also easy for a man to disappear to the Railway Line or cross the border into Angola. Many men who were alleged to have *kaliloze* guns did so and thus escaped investigation.'

In the same report, the apparently large number of *kaliloze* gunmen from the sub-districts (*kutas*) of Tuuwa and Litulilo is also noted.

TABLE 6

Kaliloze gunmen; Tuuwa and Litulilo *kutas*, Kalabo district

KUTA	NO. OF KALILOZE GUNMEN	ADULT MALES	TOTAL POPULATION
Tuuwa	20	2,417	8,767
Litulilo	18	1,743	5,950

'although the population of these two *kuta* areas (particularly of Tuuwa) is high, the necessity for as many as 20 or 18 executioners in one *kuta* area is not at all clear.' Although for one per cent or less of the adult male population to indulge in witchdoctoring is not an unusually high percentage, these figures do give some indication of the popularity of this weapon.

Almost all those sent to prison as a result of the investigations have now been released, and life in Barotseland is much the same as it was before. Practitioners may be less willing to publicize their activities, and some may even have given up entirely. This is perhaps a good thing, though those who have all along felt strongly that the Courts were taking away from them not only their enemies, the *baloi*, but also their defenders, the *ng'aka*, will no doubt disagree.

[1] Kalabo district files, 1957.

Distribution

Mongu and Senanga districts between them contain most of the Barotse plain; Kalabo contains the remainder, while Sesheke and Mankoya are cut off from it. The first two districts together provided roughly eighty per cent of the total cases, while the third provided most of the remainder. Sesheke and, at the time, Mankoya provided only negligible quantities.

It is tempting to consider that these two facts are related, and to conclude either that the plain contains a much greater number of magicians, or that its inhabitants proved more susceptible to the wave of hysteria that swept through the Protectorate. A careful examination of the distribution (using *kuta* areas as the spatial unit) of cases throughout the four riverine districts, however, fails to lend any support to these theories and, in fact, demonstrates that the geographical separation of plain and bush is of no consequence in this context. No fixed distribution pattern can be traced, and the conclusions drawn are that the distribution is governed, not by environmental factors, but by administrative ones. It bears no visible relationship to the distribution of magicians or to the extent of their neighbours' fears, but rather to the amount and extent of the information available to the investigating officers and to the success attendant upon their work. Each allegation investigated produced others which had in turn to be examined. Thus, in Kalabo, we find that by far the greatest number of cases came from the *kuta* areas of Tuuwa, Litulilo and, to a lesser extent, Lutwi. Close to the junction of the boundaries of these three *kuta* areas stands Sihole Mission, from which were reported the rumours that began the whole investigation. Attention was, therefore, focussed from the very beginning on these *kutas*.

The general trend of distribution by district is borne out by an examination of the distribution of cases relating to each practice. The only notable exceptions are those relating to the use of *kaliloze* guns and of *sikuyeti* and to the wearing of needle charms. These are as shown in Table 7 opposite.

Needle wearing was first noted at Kalabo, early in the investigations, and was believed to be closely connected with *kaliloze* guns and with other harmful practices. Close attention was, therefore, paid to the practice until it was realized that this connection was not really so close, nor the practice so harmful. As a result, those records that contain references to needles date mostly from the early months of the investigations and, since these began in Kalabo, a greater proportion of its records contain such references. Only Mongu records a greater number ; this is to be expected for a much greater number of cases was dealt with in this district.

TABLE 7

Cases relating to needles, *kaliloze* and *sikuyeti*

CASES RELATING TO	KALABO	MONGU	SENANGA	SESHEKE	TOTAL
Needles	82	94	4	17	197
kaliloze and *sikuyeti*	43	23	14	1	81

The use of *kaliloze* guns was also first noted in Kalabo and, as may be seen from the above figures, the number of cases involving *kaliloze* guns heard in this district exceeded those heard throughout the whole of the rest of the Protectorate. It has been argued that *kaliloze* doctors realizing, after the first few cases in Kalabo, that the magistrates viewed their weapons with considerable disapproval and that possession of them was highly incriminating, hid them carefully or even threw them away. Although some doctors and gunmen are known to have done one of these two things, the argument is not completely satisfactory for it would apply equally in Kalabo as well as in other districts. Moreover, in the general unrest, *kaliloze* doctors and gunmen were the first and most important targets of the informers and accusers. That a man had thrown his gun away or had hidden it was of little avail, when witnesses were available to testify to his once having possessed it. A more likely explanation is that the *kaliloze* being a LUNDA-LUVALE weapon, its user would find a much more receptive audience in Kalabo, with its very heavy population and considerable number of LUNDA-LUVALE. Further, since Kalabo provides the bulk of the Wenela labour force taken from the Protectorate, the link with the Witwatersrand mines would be much stronger, and the raw material for new type *kaliloze* guns obtainable more easily and in greater quantities through returning workers.

Tribal Distribution

The various tribes of the Protectorate and their groupings are given in Chapter I together with details, where available, of their size. Gluckman (1941. Chart 8) noted that certain tribes were re-

143

puted by the Lozi to specialize in particular magical practices. It is, therefore, of interest to examine the case records in the light of these specializations. Unfortunately, comparisons are only possible for four practices.

TABLE 8

Tribal specialization

PRACTICE	ACCORDING TO GLUCKMAN (1941)	ACCORDING TO CASE RECORDS, 1956/7
Rainmaking	Mbunda (Old and New), Mashi	Primarily Lozi, Kwandi and Kwangwa; Mashi are represented by only one case record
Leeches	Luvale, Kwangwa, Makoma and Totela	Primarily Lozi, Kwandi and Kwangwa
Diviners	Kwangwa and Mbunda	Primarily Kwangwa and Mbunda, but Lozi, Kwandi, Luvale, Luchazi, Nkoya and Totela are also strongly represented
Magicians*	Kwangwa, Makoma, Mbunda and Totela	Primarily Mbunda and Imilangu (Ndundulu) (the latter almost entirely from Kalabo)

* These are assumed to be witchdoctors.

While case records cannot be relied on to show a fully accurate distribution of practices, they do give a fair indication of specializations. Perhaps the most interesting points that arise from the above comparison are :

The confirmation of the tribal specializations of the Kwangwa and Mbunda in leechcraft, divining and witchdoctoring.

The lack of representation, among the case records, of rainmakers and magicians of the Mashi and the Makoma respectively.

The importance of LUYANA tribes, especially of Lozi, in present-day magical practices.

Obviously, the larger the tribe, the greater the possibility of its being strongly represented in the case records. It is, therefore, of interest to note, from the tribal census figures given in Chapter I, that the Lozi (50,811), Kwangwa (37,696), and Mbunda (32,985) are by far the largest tribes in the Protectorate. The importance of these three tribes in magical practices, as shown by their numerical strength in case records, is understandable.

The LUNDA-LUVALE tribes are often considered to be more prone to witchcraft practices than are other tribes. A count of all case records tended to confirm this impression though, in view of the small percentage of the total population to which these records refer, this confirmation must be treated with caution.

An examination of the records relating to each practice provides some interesting and often unexpected results. Thus records of necrophagy, a practice usually associated with LUNDA-LUVALE, show that, while the Luvale furnished 11 and the Mbunda 15 of the 61 cases, the three LUYANA tribes—Lozi, Kwangwa and Mbowe, contributed 17 and the NKOYA, 6.[1]

Similarly, the *kaliloze* gun is considered a LUNDA-LUVALE weapon, yet the Imilangu, a relatively small tribe, is represented in 16 of the 73 cases, more than any other tribe, while other ASSIMILATED LUYANA and LUYANA tribes are as well represented as are any of the LUNDA-LUVALE tribes. It may be concluded that acculturation has been particularly successful in this field. On the other hand, cases of *sikuyeti* are few (9 altogether) and are restricted to the LUYANA and ASSIMILATED LUYANA among whom the practice probably originated. The figures are negligible in all cases.

Of the 197 records concerned with the wearing of needle charms, the Lozi (24), Kwangwa (16), Imilangu (30, all from Kalabo), Mbunda (19) and Luvale (22) provide the bulk. The practice is fairly evenly distributed among all tribal groups.

49 of the 92 cases of rain and lightning control are provided by the LUYANA tribes, and 21 of the remainder by ASSIMILATED LUYANA though, as has been noted earlier, the Mashi provided only one case. The LUNDA-LUVALE are poorly represented; the Luvale furnish 3 cases of lightning control, the Mbunda 2 cases of rain control.

The 175 cases of witchdoctoring are fairly evenly distributed throughout all groups and, while the Mbunda and Imilangu each with 21 cases are the most important, no tribe is outstanding.

Similarly, the 172 cases of herbal doctoring are distributed throughout all groups, though the Kwangwa (32), Lozi (27) and Mbunda (29) furnish most of the cases.

[1] The bulk of the Nkoya are in Mankoya district, where a large number of cases of alleged necrophagy were heard late in 1958.

The Kwangwa provide 118 and the Mbunda 113 of the 544 cases of divining. The Lozi (48), Kwandi (30), Luvale (62), Luchazi (22), Nkoya (21) and Totela (20) contribute most of the remainder. Further investigation into the distribution of each of the various divining devices produced little of note, mainly because the samples available were small.

Of the 96 cases concerning divining baskets, it was to be expected that the Old Mbunda and LUNDA-LUVALE together should provide the majority. It is of interest to note, however, that 15 cases concerned tribes of other groups; an indication that the device is being taught to foreigners. The complicated working of the basket method probably hinders its acceptance by non-LUNDA-LUVALE diviners. It has certainly not been accepted as readily as has the *kaliloze* gun.

The Kwangwa, providing 81 of the 209 cases, appear to be the main exponents of the art of throwing the bones. The practice is fairly widespread among most tribes, and a few cases occur even among the Luvale and Mbunda. The Lozi (23), Kwandi (13) and Totela (15) also practise this method.

Only 38 cases of divining with pointing devices were recorded. Most appear to concern divining horns and, if any conclusions can be drawn from such low figures, the practice would seem to be most popular among the LUYANA tribes.

Records of divining with revolving devices number 53. The Mbunda, Luvale and Luchazi account for 38 of these, while 45 of the devices employed concern the *ngombo ya kakolokolo* device; this is mentioned in all of the above 38 records.

Reflecting (37), magnetic (52) and communication (26) methods provide too few records for satisfactory analysis. These records are scattered among the various groups, and one can only note that the Kwangwa, Mbunda and Luvale provide the majority.

Pleas

The most striking feature is the overwhelming number of pleas of Guilty that were made. Whilst, in the majority of cases, the accused had obviously been guilty of magical practices and there was material evidence to prove this, many confessed to crimes that had never been committed, to murders that had obviously been natural deaths, to eating corpses that on exhumation proved to be still intact. One would have thought that an accused, whether he were guilty or not, would plead Not Guilty and try to give some perfectly innocent explanation of the uses to which he put his equipment. Or, failing this, if the equipment were obviously magical, then to deny ownership and claim that the evidence had been 'planted' on him.

An accused who knew himself to be guilty no doubt persuaded himself to plead so for one of a variety of reasons.[1] Fear of the magistrate or of the whole machinery of the boma court, with its expert witnesses who had, during such a short period, handled so much witchcraft material, would influence some. Others obviously felt considerable pride in demonstrating their skill and ingenuity to such an attentive audience. Many probably regarded imprisonment as one of the normal risks of the profession, just as do prostitutes in England regard a periodic appearance in a magistrate's court. Yet others, numbed and hardly realizing the consequences, must have resigned themselves to their fate, telling the truth when required. Not all took matters so calmly, preferring to seek escape through suicide.

What, however, of those cases where neighbours' accusations, subsequently proved to be false, are accepted by the accused and confession made? Such cases most frequently concern witches, sorcerers and necrophagers. It is difficult to find any reason for such confessions, other than that the accused is actually persuaded of his guilt by his neighbours. The social stigma that is attached to such a person is very great, though its main effects are felt only for a short while. No wonder, therefore, that the accused prefers to acknowledge his guilt and to look for a means of expiation. Would his appearance in the courts and a spell in prison be considered to provide this?

This acquiescence and willing acceptance of neighbours' condemnation are by no means new phenomena in central Africa. One has only to read Richards' (1935) paper on the *mucapi* practices of the 1930's to realize this. This recent large-scale demonstration does, however, serve to emphasize that the influence of the witchfinder is as strong as ever, and that he still plays a very important part in the life of a native village.

Courts Wherein Tried

Almost all persons were tried in the district in which they resided and in which they were registered for tax purposes. It is significant that there was no case involving a person normally resident outside Barotseland, either elsewhere in Northern Rhodesia or in another

[1] Discussed already in Chapter II.

territory.[1] Further, although itinerant doctors and diviners are known to exist, there were few cases where such an accused was prosecuted outside his home district. This could be either because such itinerants, at the start of the investigations, felt it wiser to go home or, more feasibly, because their numbers are much less than had previously been supposed.

In contrast, 9 of the 61 accused of necrophagy (15 per cent), were charged outside their home district, although again all were residents of Barotseland. One wonders whether this is a reflection of hostility towards foreigners, especially since necrophagy is so easily confessed to, and the only material evidence is the negative one of a missing body.

Sex

The position occupied by women, in matters of magic and witchcraft, appears to be very minor. Only in cases of necrophagy and witchcraft (*baloi*) are their numbers of any significance.

TABLE 9

baloi : male and female

CASES	MALES	FEMALES	TOTAL
Necrophagy	12	49	61
Witchcraft and sorcery (*baloi*)	59	69	128

They appear to be most commonly associated with anti-social practices, just as they were in Europe in former times. Conversely, very few women are accepted or try to act as defenders of society against the *baloi*. Only in the field of herbal doctoring, where they possess certain special skills and advantages over men, is there any opening for them. Even here, only 5 females were noted among 172 records of herbal doctoring.

A very small number of female diviners was noted. The only tentative conclusion drawn is that, although a few may use divining bones, they appear to restrict themselves to the simpler devices and do not employ the more complicated pattern techniques.

Occupation

The information provided here is largely negative. With very few exceptions the accused were ordinary villagers, neither wage-earning

---

[1] Aliens resident in Northern Rhodesia require a residence permit. The court would record the place of residence rather than of origin. Thus a Zulu diviner/doctor, who came to Barotseland from Natal some seventeen years ago, is noted as a resident of Barotseland.

employees,[1] independent traders nor middlemen. As villagers, they would be employed in domestic and agricultural pursuits, fishing, hunting, cattle-minding and the like and, on occasions, working at some specialist craft, such as woodcarving or ironworking. There would, therefore, be plenty of opportunity for personal relations between themselves and their neighbours to become strained, and little chance of their going away on business from the village to allow such tension to slacken.

Rank/Position

Information available on *indunas* is again negative, though for a different reason. To accuse a chief or *induna* of witchcraft practices is impolitic, not from the magical but from the rational viewpoint, because of the power such a person wields. In Barotseland, where traditional forms of government are less decayed than they are elsewhere in the territory, respect for such power is still great. It may be supposed, however, that such highly placed people are little different in their beliefs and practices from their neighbours.

Headmen would appear to lack this respect and protection. An examination of the data provides some interesting points, for while, for most practices, the percentage of headmen accused ranges between 12 per cent and 17 per cent, for some practices it is much higher.

Headmen are usually still in their prime and still receiving a good share of the food coming into the village. It is to be expected, therefore, that few charges of necrophagy should have been made against them, especially since, as will be shown later, victims are usually the close kin of the necrophager, and since a headman is very dependent upon such kin for support in the village. In fact, of the 61 cases of necrophagy only one concerns a headman.

Of case records of witchcraft and sorcery (*baloi*) 10 per cent relate to headmen. This is at first sight an average return. When one considers only male accused, however, the proportion rises to 22 per cent. Accusations of sorcery often reflect tensions and hostility that have grown from non-magical causes. It is reasonable to suppose that accusations against headmen often result from conflicts over land and authority, and provide the excuse for a member or section of his village to break away. The headman may also try to frighten his opponents by claiming magical powers or even try to destroy them with sorcery.

[1] Returned migrant labourers are noted in case records as villagers, not employees.

Again, headmen are the accused in 21 of the 92 cases of weather control. This high proportion probably stems from the desire that must be present in almost every headman to protect his village and its inhabitants from harm. If at the same time his prestige is increased, this is an added benefit. Conversely, a man who is able to drive away lightning and to call up rain when required, is much more likely to attract and keep adherents to his new village. There is insufficient data in the case records to separate raindoctors, who *control* the elements, from laymen, who merely drive away lightning from their own villages or call rain to them. One wonders, however, to which group these headmen belong. A man who is reputed to be able to direct lightning to or withhold rain from a specific place, is likely to make enemies as well as friends. The few indications that exist in the records suggest that such a man does not usually become a headman. The data on this point is, however, inadequate for any firm conclusions to be drawn.

Of the 96 diviners using divining baskets, 22 were headmen. It is perhaps reasonable to suppose that the qualities required of a successful headman are similar to those required of a basket diviner. Both demand skill and some intelligence, as well as personality and the ability to catch and to hold the attention and confidence of others. Other divining devices that are but 'gimmicks' to gain popular interest do not require all of these and, as far as intelligence is concerned, may even require the opposite.

Necrophagers and Their Victims

Necrophagers are believed to hold feasts at which three, four or more of them consume a corpse supplied by each in turn. Assuming that such a group of necrophagers was of three persons, then each might be expected to supply one-third of the total corpses consumed. If the groups were larger, the fraction would, of course, be smaller. Of the 61 victims noted in Table 10a, 19, roughly one-third, have been identified by accused necrophagers as kinsfolk. From this one may reasonably suppose that, if full records were available, it would be possible to trace a kinship relationship between each of the 61 victims and the particular necrophager said to have produced the corpse at the feast. This agrees with the belief that necrophagers prey on their kin. Conversely, the more rational deduction may be made that accusations of necrophagy are usually made against kin ; another instance of hostility and tension within a small group being brought into the open, and one of the parties being arraigned on a charge of anti-social activities.

It will also be seen from Table 10a that a necrophager selects his victim from his own or a junior generation, preferring especially the second generation below his own. Since most necrophagers are well over fifty years of age, the absence of victims from senior generations is understandable. That four of the five cases involving victims of the same generation concern spouses, is similarly understandable when one bears in mind the latent hostility and suspicion that exist between relatives-in-law, and how these become active at the death of one of the partners to the marriage. Again, that necrophagers should be considered to have a taste for children (Table 10b), is an understandable belief. The mortality rate for young children in an African community is high and the diviner cannot be blamed too harshly for finding, for the bereaved parents, a more acceptable explanation than that the child died from an unknown ailment. The aged in the group are convenient scapegoats.

It is surprising that co-wives and their offspring have not been mentioned as being either victims or necrophagers. One would have thought that the relationship, so often one of hostility, would be ideal for such accusations. Perhaps the records err by their omission, or include them with kin.

Table 10
Necrophagers and their victims

a. *Relationship of each necrophager to the corpse he had eaten*
   Generation of the victim

SENIOR	OWN	FIRST JUNIOR	SECOND JUNIOR	TOTAL	OTHERS AND UNKNOWN	TOTAL
—	5	3	11	19	42	61

b. *Age group of victims*

ADULTS	CHILDREN	TOTAL	UNKNOWN	TOTAL
12	20	32	29	61

Needles

As will be seen from Table 11a, almost all needles recorded were simple lengths of actual needles, probably gramophone or sewing needles. Most needles are worn singly. In some cases, more than one has been found in a person's body, perhaps indicating contact with dangerous magical elements or a serious illness, such as tuberculosis.

TABLE 11

Needles

a. *Types and materials*

METAL NEEDLES	BONE	HORN	NAILS	TOTAL
193	I	I	2	197

b. *Number worn*

ONE	TWO	MORE THAN TWO	TOTAL
179	6	12	197

c. *Position on body*

	RIGHT	LEFT	UNKNOWN	TOTAL
Chest	5	10	100	115
Back	I	I	I	3
Arms	I	2	—	3
Unknown	—	—	76	76
Total	7	13	177	197

The accepted place for a needle is the chest and, where a record has been kept, it almost invariably states that the insertion took place in this part of the body, though usually it does not state on which side. A few cases have been noted of needles being worn elsewhere in the body; these are restricted to the back or to the arms. It is reasonable to assume that of the 76 needles, the positions of which were not recorded, most were inserted in the chest. Any variation in position from this would, most probably, have been recorded by the magistrate. Whether the chest was chosen merely for convenience, or whether there is any connection with chest ailments, is not known.

Table 12 shows, in five-year groups, the estimated ages of the accused when tried. Any conclusions on age or year of initiation or, stemming from these, on the average length of practices or annual number of initiations should be drawn with caution. In such matters, these figures can but indicate possible trends, rather than demonstrate concrete movements.

The Muloi and the Necrophager

A comparison of the age ranges of these two anti-social practices is of interest. Disregarding an isolated case from the 25+ age group, the age range for both practices is from 35 to 70+. The majority of both groups is from the over 50s but, whereas the peak for the former is reached immediately after this age, that for the latter is not reached

TABLE 12
Age groups

	BELOW 25	25+	30+	35+	40+	45+	50+	55+	60+	65+	70+	UNKNOWN	TOTAL
Muloi	—	1	—	3	5	14	25	15	26	20	18	1	128
Necrophager	—	—	—	1	2	4	8	9	17	12	8	—	61
Witchdoctor	—	3	10	35	27	37	21	14	17	5	5	1	175
Herbal doctor	—	1	8	21	17	34	23	24	20	19	3	2	172
Rain and Lightning doctor	—	—	2	7	6	13	16	21	13	9	5	—	92
Kaliloze and *sikuyeti*	—	1	8	20	13	16	8	5	7	1	2	—	81
Needles	—	4	6	25	19	16	14	23	16	10	6	58	197
Diviner–general	1	3	21	55	51	85	83	73	71	59	36	6	544
Divining devices:													
Baskets	—	2	3	3	4	11	18	12	21	15	6	1	96
Bones	—	—	5	20	16	35	30	34	25	24	17	3	209
Pointing	—	—	1	4	5	5	7	6	5	6	—	1	38
Revolving	—	—	2	3	7	14	8	5	7	5	1	1	53
Reflecting	—	1	3	7	6	5	6	3	1	4	—	1	37
Magnetic	1	—	1	3	4	7	6	6	6	10	8	—	52
Communication	—	—	1	5	4	6	2	2	2	2	1	1	26
Treatment	—	—	2	4	1	3	2	1	2	—	—	—	13
Ordeal	—	—	—	—	1	—	—	—	—	—	—	—	1
Unidentified	—	—	8	17	14	15	10	11	3	6	4	1	89
Suicides and attempted suicides	—	—	—	—	1	1	1	1	1	—	—	22	27

till 60+. The secondary peak of the *muloi* at 60+ probably reflects that of the necrophager and is indicative of combined practices. After 60+, the decline is probably due to deaths rather than to the cessation of practice but, even at 70+, there is still a number in both groups still practising.

That these practices should be associated with the aged and senile is to be expected. At 50, a Bantu man or woman is a generation above those in their prime, is usually a grandparent and is growing more and more of a burden on, and less and less an economic asset to the group. His or her children are more concerned with their own offspring and fortunes. The aged are regarded as being close to death; frequently in fact, their spouses are dead. Senility must be common, as must also be the eccentricity of behaviour that provokes suspicion and witchcraft accusations.

The Ng'aka and the Sitondo

Both witchdoctors and herbal doctors reach their peak much earlier in life than do the *muloi* and the necrophager. This is to be expected; a successful doctor must be in full possession of his wits though, at the same time, adult enough to gain and hold the respect of his audience. A raindoctor has less need of his brain. His profession requires belief in his own ability, and the performance of rituals, dances and songs. The peak at 55+ is, therefore, understandable. At this age, the peak is past for the witchdoctors and herbal doctors and there is a decline in their numbers. This can be attributed to failing powers to hold audiences or to act decisively. Raindoctors decline in numbers more slowly and, even at 70+, are relatively more numerous than their colleagues.

A question that these figures raise is whether, by the age of 35 or 40, a man feels that he should already have made his mark in the world in some sphere, by holding either a headmanship or some similar position of respect. Do men turn to witchdoctoring at this time in order to obtain such a position or to improve, even further, their social status? A comparative study of the social positions and lay pursuits of a selected number of *ng'aka* would be very interesting and might throw further light on why men take up these practices.

Diviners

An examination of the figures for types of divining devices shows that of the two most popular devices, the basket and the bones, the latter reaches its peak number of practitioners some five years before the former. In fact, the former diviners do not reach their peak till the age of 60+. This may be because of the intricacy of the device and the length of time required to master it. Of other devices some, such as reflecting, treating, communication and ordeal, reach an early peak, while others, such as pointing and magnetic, reach it rather late. Of all these minor devices, only magnetic is still being practised to any extent by men over the age of 70.

Tables 13 and 14

Table 13a deals with those feasts on human flesh that have been confessed by necrophagers. Most of the cases date from the last decade, and the majority from post-1952. This may be interpreted either as a recent increase in practice, or merely as a means of explaining the fates of various individuals who have died in the last few years.

Table 13b shows the years when witchdoctors began their practices, and again there is a marked increase after 1952. For both tables, it may be said that the years, 1955 and 1956, were peak years.

Table 14 compares the ages of needle wearers at their trials with their ages when the needles were inserted. It would appear that most needles are inserted in youth or early prime, and that the frequency of insertion decreases in inverse proportion to age, falling off steeply after the age of 59. This is perhaps either because an old man or woman is too poor to afford the fee for the operation or is considered to stand in less need of such protection from malignant magic. It will be seen that the age at insertion is some five or ten years earlier than the age at trial. This would suggest that the *year* of insertion, rather than the *age* of insertion, is likely to be of the greater interest.

Table 13c shows the year of insertion of needles. The practice is old, as is confirmed by the decayed state of some of the older needles when extracted. Lewanika's death in 1916 is a useful, commonly accepted date which serves for comparative chronology; no needles were apparently inserted before that year. In or about 1950, the practice began to grow more popular and, in 1953, reached a peak of popularity at which it remained for the following two years. In 1956, it began to decline, probably because of the investigations.

These tables indicate that in or about 1953 interest in witchcraft appeared to increase. Whether this indication is the product of a poor sample is uncertain. If it is not, then one must seek a cause of this increased activity, a cause that probably dates from the early 1950's.

TABLE 13

Necrophagers, witchdoctors and needles

	PRE-1920	1920s	1930s	1940	1941	1942	1943	1944	1945	1946	1947	1948	1949	1950	1951	1952	1953	1954	1955	1956	1957	UNKNOWN	TOTAL
a. Necrophager— year of feast or of last feast	—	—	—	—	—	—	—	—	1	—	1	1	3	1	1	1	6	4	6	8	1	27	61
b. Witchdoctor— year of beginning practice	3	3	3	—	—	1	2	—	4	1	2	6	2	2	3	7	12	11	28	19	2	54	175
c. Needles— year of insertion	8	8	16	1	4	4	2	5	7	2	5	4	2	7	7	9	13	13	13	9	2	57	198

156

TABLE 14

Needle wearers. Age at trial: Age at insertion

Age at insertion

Age at insertion	Age at trial											UNKNOWN	TOTAL
	BELOW 25	25+	30+	35+	40+	45+	50+	55+	60+	65+	70+		
70+											1		1
65+											1		1
60+									1	1	1		3
55+								6		3			9
50+							1	2	4	1	1		9
45+						3	7	3	3		1		17
40+					6	5	3		3	1‡			18
35+				6	4	3	1	2	1		1		18
30+			2	9	4	2	1	4	1				23
25+		2	2	4	3	2	1	1		3			18
20+		1	2	3		1		2	2	1‡			12
15+		1		1	1			3	1				7
Below 15				2*	1†								3
Unknown												59	59
Total	—	4	6	25	19	16	14	23	16	10	6	59	198

* Age 12 and 13 years respectively.   † Age 9 years.   ‡ Man with two needles.

Suicides and Attempted Suicides

These numbered 27, and were distributed between the four districts in much the same proportions as were the witchcraft cases. Only one attempt proved unsuccessful; whether this was because of the method chosen or whether other failures passed unnoticed is unknown. All but one of the cases occurred in the home district of the person concerned, and all cases concerned Barotse residents, not foreigners.

There was a fairly even balance between the sexes, 15 males and 12 females. Possibly, the high proportion of females may be taken to mean that most accusations were of practising black rather than white magic. The number of headmen involved amounted to 7 per cent, rather a low figure but probably because the sample was small. No chiefs or *indunas*, and only 2 headmen, were involved. The remaining cases concerned ordinary villagers, neither employees nor independent businessmen.

All but three of the suicides are known to have acted through fear of being accused of, or arrested for witchcraft practices. The rest probably feared such arrest but, while available information points to this fact, the magistrate was not sufficiently sure that he could record it as the actual cause. That the desire for escape from what must have appeared an impossible situation was very strong, is shown by the fact that seven of the intending suicides escaped from custody in order to kill themselves.

The method most frequently employed, both by males and females, was hanging. This was used in 23 cases. Poison was used on only one occasion. The unsuccessful attempt recorded was that of a female who tried to drown herself. This was the only instance noted of the use of drowning for this purpose. The remaining two suicides cut their throats.

Conclusion

The conclusions drawn in this chapter must be treated more as tentative indications than as definite statements for, as has been emphasized throughout, the statistics on which they are based are by no means completely satisfactory. Even so, these conclusions are still of interest.

The very wide distribution of, to use the term in its widest sense, witchcraft beliefs and practices has been clearly demonstrated. This distribution is both geographical and tribal. Popular local belief that neighbours of other tribes are more pre-occupied with the super-natural than are the people of one's own tribe, is not really confirmed ; while the ascription of particular practices and devices only to parti-cular tribes is no longer correct, as a result of culture contact and the rapid diffusion that is today possible.

The practitioners themselves are also of interest. As may be ex-pected, rank, position and occupation have little effect on a man's be-liefs. Should he be a practising doctor, diviner or raindoctor, how-ever, his political status may, to a certain extent, be affected. Some practices would appear to debar a man from village headmanship ; others would appear to be associated with the office. Much, it would seem, depends on the extent of his supposed powers and on his use or potential misuse of them. There are surprisingly few itinerant doc-tors and diviners but a significant percentage of foreigners accused of anti-social activities. There is also a significant percentage of females among those suspected of indulging in such activities, and a negligible number who divine or act as doctors.

Certain accepted ideas regarding necrophagy, such as that the *muloi* preys on his relatives and especially on children, are reflected in the case records. It is a great pity that no study of the reasons and motives behind actual accusations of witchcraft, nor even an analysis of more than a few of the letters of accusation was possible. Such a study would, undoubtedly, have provided much valuable data.

Although the age range of those involved in each practice has been examined separately, it is possible to summarize the conclu-sions. Briefly, it would seem that anti-social practices are associated more with the aged, while those of benefit to the community are, with certain exceptions, carried on by men in their prime. The simpler magical practices, those that make few demands on intelligence and require little more than a firm belief in one's own powers, may be continued till quite a late age. Pattern divining too is surprisingly popular among the older members of the community. One would have thought that the advancing years and the resultant slowing down of the diviner's mental processes would have seriously im-paired his divining ability. In considering these age ranges one must, of course, bear in mind that the African is living in a rapidly changing society. What appears today to be a practice favoured by the aged may, in the past, have been carried on by those in their prime. Changing fashions may have caused a substantial reduction in the numbers of those entering a particular profession, leaving only those who were already exponents to continue the practice.

From the three parts of Table 13 emerges the suggestion that the supposed practice of necrophagy, the insertion of needle charms, and the initiation of witchdoctors each reached a peak during the period, 1953 to 1956; in other words, during the years immediately preceding the investigations. If this actually occurred, and is not a peculiarity produced by the statistics themselves or by the way in which they were gathered, it would be most interesting to seek the reasons for the increased activity.

The number of suicides that occurred during and perhaps as a result of the investigations serves to emphasize the importance of magic and witchcraft in the everyday life of the African. One may conclude that, while the disturbance created by the investigations has long since died down, accusations of witchcraft still continue to be made and that, beneath the apparently calm surface, there is a turmoil of activity, of suspicions and fears that cannot be quieted or controlled by means of normal legal processes.

CHAPTER VIII

CONCLUSION

I n the Preface, the primary aim of this book was said to be the description of the witchcraft and allied practices and beliefs of the peoples of Barotseland. This, it is hoped, has now been done and, at the same time, the importance of the roles of the three leading characters, the *muloi*, the *ng'aka*, and the *mulauli*, demonstrated. One must not, however, forget the supporting cast, the clients. Without their assistance and faith in magic, the machinations of the leading characters would be but empty gestures, their fine or fierce words mere fantasies, and their behaviour open to ridicule. Indeed, without the client the drama could not go on, for not only does he act in the play but he also finances it and even provides the plot.

The witchcraft beliefs of the peoples of Barotseland have been noticeably affected by the contacts they have, mainly as migrant workers, with other tribes and with modern urban culture. Even so, village life follows much the same pattern that it has always done and, below the surface, lies always the fear of witchcraft and of the unknown. This fear rises often to the surface and accusations of witchcraft or of sorcery are frequently made, for everyone is a potential *muloi* and any unusual occurrence caused perhaps by magic. While strangers and foreigners are especially suspect, relatives too are not exempt, for *baloi* are believed to prey particularly on the members of their own families. Those too, such as witchdoctors and raindoctors, who are considered to possess special magical powers are also suspect for, even though they employ these powers to protect others, they may still in secret use them to cause harm.

One must view these fears and suspicions in their social context. Beliefs in witchcraft and in supernatural intervention provide an acceptable explanation of the causes of misfortune and indeed of anything mysterious or inexplicable by normal means. Faith in the ability of the diviner to indicate the appropriate cause of his present trouble gives a man something definite on which to focus his fears. Where a witch is indicated, he is able to give actual expression to them, especially since the diviner is frequently but confirming an existing feeling of hostility and suspicion. Faith in the ability of the *ng'aka* to control these mysterious malignant forces gives the ordinary villager, dependent on the vagaries of the weather for his precarious existence and able to cure only the simplest of the ills to which he is subject, a reason for his existence and the confidence to carry on living.

Most, if not all primitive peoples in the world believe in witchcraft and magic, and these beliefs are surprisingly similar. Whether there has been any diffusion of ideas from one continent to another, and whether these beliefs are vestiges of early religions or fertility cults are problems that are too wide to be discussed here. It is reasonable though to accept that diffusion has occurred within the Bantu-speaking group of tribes, and that there should be a general similarity of beliefs and practices throughout Africa, south of the Sahara, and a more particular one among groups of tribes of the same immediate origin or occupying the same region. Even so, there is still plenty of room left for divergence between individual tribes. Barotse beliefs and practices, however, show a surprising homogeneity which is a tribute to the ease of communication between different tribes and between different areas, and also to the receptivity of the inhabitants to foreign ideas. Certain groups still specialize in particular practices, but these are gradually being adopted by their neighbours.

The more dynamic cultures of the LUNDA-LUVALE have, in a relatively short space of time, had a profound effect on those of the LUYANA and of the other tribes of the Protectorate, and their influence may be expected to continue and to increase. At the same time, counter-diffusion is occurring, and the LUNDA-LUVALE will themselves absorb much from their neighbours. The final result will, no doubt, be homogeneity of culture and beliefs.

Diffusion is a most interesting cultural phenomenon which is both selective and erratic in its behaviour. An excellent example is provided by the Kololo period of Barotse history. These foreign invaders, speaking a completely different form of Bantu language, differing from their subjects not only in beliefs but even in their concepts of life, and disappearing from the scene after only a few decades, have left their mark on Barotse culture. Besides their language, they have also left some of their magical beliefs and methods. The importation of divining bones has been discussed in Chapter IV. It is probable that they were responsible for introducing the practice of raindoctoring and the belief in the lightning bird. Possibly too, some Barotse ordeals and fertility beliefs owe something to the Kololo.

CONCLUSION

The Barotse not only accept new ideas, they also give them to others outside their borders, especially eastward to the Tonga and the Ila. Divining bones again afford an excellent illustration.

Cultures are dynamic and not static. Witchcraft beliefs and practices, indeed the very bases of these, are subject to changes in the face of new pressures and conditions. In this century, the greatest pressure has resulted from the presence of the European. Under his influence, the African has been compelled to recognize the importance of monetary wealth ; his social and political behaviour have been, to a certain extent, restricted ; he has had to leave unharmed those whom he believes are his enemies, the *baloi*. He may no longer burn them ; he may not even accuse them. The traditional values of his tribe are losing their meaning for him ; skills that were once proud possessions are no longer of use, their products discarded in favour of mass-produced goods from the stores. Village life breaks up as young men move away to the towns in search of the money to buy these goods, or in order to escape traditional obligations. Those who remain are left with the shell of their former culture and, as yet, nothing with which to replace it. Hunter (1936) has examined the problems and tensions caused by this breakdown of the old cultures, and has noted the African's resultant belief that witchcraft practices are on the increase. The modern *mahamba* of the LUNDA-LUVALE are similar mechanisms for relieving the tension caused in the individual by the stresses and strains of his present existence.

On a different level, European influence makes itself felt in the material culture of the magician. He is compelled to adapt his methods so that they are more acceptable to his changing clientele. During the early stages of the investigations, considerable interest was taken in the use of the needle charm and of the modern *kaliloze* gun. The former was almost certainly influenced by European practices ; the latter may be considered the unfortunate result of an attempt to bring a traditional weapon up to date. Its development and employment should not be misread as anything more sinister. Neither should the men who brought it into Barotseland be considered to have absorbed, during their stay in the towns, anything more harmful than the magical beliefs and ideas of other tribes. These, together with any novel witchcraft devices, they eagerly brought back to their villages. Their own beliefs, however, remained intact and they appear to have slipped easily into their old cultural environment.

163

The *kaliloze* gun and the needle charm are minor devices employed in witchcraft and should be viewed as such, while the effect of the visits made by migrant workers to the outside world may be considered to have touched only the fringe and not the core of Barotse witchcraft beliefs.

The Laws of Northern Rhodesia[1] are very widely framed in order to cover the whole field of magical practices and there is no doubt that they do this admirably, the only omissions being cannibalism and necrophagy. All other practices, from sorcery down to the possession of charms, are covered, and indeed a case may usually be brought under any one of a number of sections of the Witchcraft Ordinance. This is reasonable where the accused is a sorcerer, witchdoctor or diviner. The ordinary layman, however, trying with a charm to protect himself against magic, not necessarily caused through witchcraft, is also guilty of an offence. The village headman too, seeking with rain charms to defend his people from a storm, is guilty ; while the herbal doctor,[2] unless he sticks strictly to material medicines, is liable to break the law. Should he slip a needle under the patient's skin to safeguard him in the future, should he in diagnosing the malady use any diving device, should he attempt to treat psychological disorders by exorcising a possessing spirit, no matter how successful his treatment he is breaking the law.

This is perhaps the weakest part of the law. It takes no cognizance of the success of or the value to the individual of his faith in his treatment. Fortunately, the interpretation of the law is left to the district officer who, provided he is adequately informed on the witchcraft beliefs of the area, is able to apply the law sensibly. Even so, the possession of a needle charm may result for the wearer in six months imprisonment with hard labour. Before another court, he may only receive a sentence of a few days.

While the Witchcraft Ordinance has a restraining influence on the behaviour of the indigenous people, it cannot be said to have made any great changes in their concepts of what is good and bad in magic, rather it has produced a certain amount of frustration. The 1956/1957 investigations will not, in the long run, have any marked effect

---

[1] See Appendix. Cases of necrophagy are usually brought under Section 111 of Cap 6, The Penal Code.

[2] It must be remembered that European medical services are very meagre. To serve the 300,000 inhabitants of Barotseland there were, at the beginning of 1957, but seven doctors and twenty-three dispensaries, of which only nine were staffed by European sisters.

on witchcraft beliefs. They must have prevented, for a time, too public a demonstration of them but that is all, and it is probable that in
stirring up old feuds and creating new enmities and distrust, they did
a certain amount of harm.

Witchcraft beliefs are too strong to be driven out by legal methods.
Rather, these should be employed as a curb, to be applied when practices become too obvious or too unrestrained. Witchcraft, for the
African, is a living force and one which still plays a very great part in
his life. No doubt, as twin standards of health and education rise, and
as he takes his place among the more civilized peoples of the world,
his interest in witchcraft will wane and the present period be seen to
be but a phase in the development of his culture.

APPENDIX

THE LAWS (Extract)
Chapter 30
WITCHCRAFT

1. This Ordinance may be cited as the Witchcraft Ordinance.

2. In this Ordinance, unless inconsistent with the context—

    'property' includes animals;

    'witchcraft' includes the throwing of bones, the use of charms and any other means, process or device adopted in the practice of witchcraft or sorcery;

    'act complained of' includes any death, injury, damage, disease or calamity, whether of an accidental or of a tortious character;

    'boiling water test' means the dipping into boiling water of the limbs or any portion of the body of a person.

3. Whoever—

    (1) names or indicates or accuses or threatens to accuse any person as being a wizard or witch; or

    (2) imputes to any person the use of non-natural means in causing any death, injury, damage or calamity; or

    (3) asserts that any person has by committing adultery caused in some non-natural way death, injury, damage or calamity;

    shall be liable upon conviction to a fine not exceeding twenty-five pounds or to imprisonment with or without hard labour for any term not exceeding one year or to both such fine and imprisonment:

    Provided that this section shall not apply to any person who makes a report to a District Officer or European police officer.

    (as amended by No. 47 of 1948 and No. 31 of 1952)

4. Whoever shall be proved to be by habit or profession a witch doctor or witch finder shall be liable upon conviction to a fine not exceeding fifty pounds or to imprisonment with or without hard labour for any term not exceeding two years or to both such fine and imprisonment.

    (as amended by No. 47 of 1948 and No. 31 of 1952)

5. Any person who—

    (i) represents himself as able by supernatural means to cause fear, annoyance, or injury to another in mind, person or property; or

(ii) pretends to exercise any kind of supernatural power, witchcraft, sorcery or enchantment calculated to cause such fear, annoyance or injury;

shall be liable to a fine not exceeding fifty pounds or to imprisonment with or without hard labour for any term not exceeding two years.

(No. 47 of 1948)

6. Whosoever shall—

(1) by the exercise of any witchcraft or any non-natural means whatsoever pretend or attempt to discover where and in what manner any property supposed or alleged to have been stolen or lost may be found or indicate any person as a thief or as the perpetrator of any crime or any other act complained of; or

(2) in the pretence of discovering or in the attempt to discover whether or not any person has committed any crime or any other act complained of administer or cause to be administered to any person with or without his consent any emetic or purgative or apply or cause to be applied to any person with or without his consent the boiling water test or any other test whatsoever; or

(3) instigate, direct, control or preside at the doing of any act specified in the foregoing part of this section;

shall be liable upon conviction to the punishments provided by section *four* hereof.

7. Whoever employs or solicits any person—

(1) to name or indicate any person as being a wizard or witch;

(2) to name or indicate by means of witchcraft or by the use of any non-natural means or by the administration of any emetic or purgative or by the application of any test whatsoever any person as the perpetrator of any alleged crime or other act complained of;

(3) to advise him or any person how by means of witchcraft or by the use of any non-natural means or by means of any emetic or purgative or test whatsoever the perpetrator of any alleged crime or other act complained of may be discovered;

(4) to advise him on any matter or for any purpose whatsoever by means of witchcraft or non-natural means;

shall be liable upon conviction to the punishments provided by section *three* hereof.

8. Any person who is present at the administration to any person of any test the administration of which is punishable under the provisions of this Ordinance shall be liable upon conviction to a fine not exceeding ten pounds or to imprisonment with or without hard labour for any term not exceeding one year or to both such fine and imprisonment:

Provided that no person called as a witness to prove the administration of any test as aforesaid shall be deemed to be an accomplice or to need corroboration as such by reason only that he was present at the administration of any test as aforesaid.

(as amended by No. 31 of 1952)

9. Whoever on the advice of any person pretending to the knowledge of witchcraft or of any non-natural processes or in the exercise of any witchcraft or of any non-natural means shall use or cause to be put into operation such means or processes as he may have been advised or may believe to be calculated to injure any person or any property shall be liable upon conviction to the punishments provided by section *four* hereof.

10. Every person professing to be able to control by non-natural means the course of nature or using any subtle craft, means or device by means of witchcraft, charms or otherwise to deceive or impose upon any other person shall be liable upon conviction to a fine not exceeding ten pounds or to imprisonment with or without hard labour for any term not exceeding one year or to both such fine and imprisonment.

(as amended by No. 31 of 1952)

11. (1) Any person who collects, makes, sells or uses or assists or takes part in collecting, selling, making or using any charm or poison or thing which he intends for use either by himself or by some other person for the purpose of any act punishable by this Ordinance shall be liable upon conviction to a fine not exceeding ten pounds or to imprisonment with or without hard labour for any term not exceeding one year or to both such fine and imprisonment.

(2) Any person who has in his possession any charm or poison or thing which he intends for use either by himself or by some other person for the purpose of any act punishable by this Ordinance shall be liable upon conviction to a fine not exceeding five pounds or to imprisonment with or without hard labour for any term not exceeding six months or to both such fine and imprisonment.

A person found in possession of anything commonly used for the purpose of an act punishable by this Ordinance shall be deemed to have intended such thing for use for the purpose of an act punishable by this Ordinance unless and until the contrary be proved.

(as amended by No. 31 of 1952)

12. Any chief or headman who directly or indirectly permits, promotes, encourages or facilitates the commission of any act punishable by this Ordinance or who knowing of such act or intended act does not forthwith report the same to the District Commissioner or a District Officer shall be liable upon conviction to a fine not exceeding fifty pounds or to imprisonment with or without hard labour for any term not exceeding three years.

13. Any person who shall receive or obtain any consideration whatsoever or the

promise thereof for or in respect of the doing by such person of any act punishable by this Ordinance shall if he has actually received such consideration be deemed guilty of the offence of obtaining by false pretences and if he has not actually received such consideration but only the promise thereof be deemed guilty of the offence of attempting to obtain by false pretences and shall be liable upon conviction to punishment accordingly.

Any agreement for the giving of any consideration for or in respect of the doing of any act punishable by this Ordinance shall be null and void.

Chapter 6

THE PENAL CODE (Extract)

Section 111

Every person who with the intention of wounding the feelings of any person or of insulting the religion of any person, or with the knowledge that the feelings of any person are likely to be wounded, or that the religion of any person is likely to be insulted thereby, commits any trespass in any place of worship or in any place of sepulture or in any place set apart for the performance of funeral rites or as a depository for the remains of the dead, or offers any indignity to any human corpse, or causes disturbance to any persons assembled for the purpose of funeral ceremonies, is guilty of a misdemeanour.

BIBLIOGRAPHY

Arnot, F. S. *Garenganze*. London, 1889.

Ashton, E. H. *Medicine, Magic and Sorcery among the Southern Sotho*. Communication from the School of African Studies, New Series, No. 10, University of Cape Town, Cape Town, 1943.

Bentley, Rev. W. Holman. *Pioneering on the Congo* (2 vols.). London, 1900.

Birket-Smith, K. *The Eskimos*. London, 1959.

Bleek, D. F. *The Naron, A Bushman tribe of the Central Kalahari*. Cambridge, 1928.

Brelsford, W. V. *The Tribes of Northern Rhodesia*. Lusaka, 1956.

Colson, E. 'Rain Shrines of the Plateau Tonga of Northern Rhodesia.' *Africa*, Vol. XVIII, 1948.
    Marriage and the Family among the Plateau Tonga of Northern Rhodesia. Manchester, 1958.
    The Social Organization of the Gwembe Tonga. Manchester, 1960.

Colson, E. and Gluckman, M. *Seven Tribes of British Central Africa*. Oxford, 1951.

Delachaux, Th. 'Méthode et instruments de divination en Angola.' *Acta Tropica*, Vol. 3, No. 2, Basel, 1946.

Doke, C. M. *The Lambas of Northern Rhodesia*. London, 1931.

Drennan, M. R. 'Two Witch-doctors' outfits from Angola.' *Bantu Studies*, Vol. VIII, No. 4, Johannesburg, 1934.

Evans-Pritchard, E. E. *Witchcraft, Oracles and Magic among the Azande*. Oxford, 1937.

Fanshawe, D. B. and Hough, C. D. 'Poisonous Plants of Northern Rhodesia.' *Forest Research Bulletin*, No. 1, Lusaka, 1960.

Federal Broadcasting Corporation. *Listeners' Letters*. 1957 (roneo).

Field, M. J. *Witchcraft as a primitive interpretation of mental disorder*. Paper read at a CCTA/CSA Specialists' Meeting on Mental Health, London, 1958 (roneo).
    Search for Security. London, 1960.

Frazer, Sir J. G. *Magic and Religion*. Thinkers' Library, No. 100, London, 1944.

Garbutt, H. W. 'Native Superstition and Witchcraft in South Africa.' *Journal of the Royal Anthropological Institute*, Vol. XXXIX, Part 2, London, 1909.

Gelfand, M. *Medicine and Magic of the Mashona*. Cape Town, 1956.

BIBLIOGRAPHY

Gilges, W. *Some African Poison Plants and Medicines of Northern Rhodesia.* Occasional Paper No. 11 of the Rhodes-Livingstone Museum, Livingstone, 1955.

Gluckman, M. *Economy of the Central Barotse Plain.* Rhodes-Livingstone Paper No. 7, Livingstone, 1941.

    'The Lozi of Barotseland in North-Western Rhodesia,' in Colson, E. and Gluckman, M., *Seven Tribes of British Central Africa.* Oxford, 1951.

    The Judicial Process among the Barotse of Northern Rhodesia. Manchester, 1955.

Gouldsbury, C. and Sheane, H. *The Great Plateau of Northern Rhodesia.* London, 1911.

Hoernlé, A. W. 'Magic and Medicine,' in Schapera, I., *The Bantu-speaking Tribes of South Africa.* London, 1937.

Hogg, G. *Cannibalism and Human Sacrifice.* London, 1958.

Hunt, N. A. 'Some Notes on Witchdoctor's Bones.' *Nada,* No. 27, Salisbury, 1950.

Hunter, M. *Reaction to Conquest.* Oxford, 1936.

Jalla, A. *The Story of the Barotse Nation* (trans. of *Litaba za Sicaba sa Malozi*). Lusaka, 1961 (roneo).

Junod, H. A. *The Life of a South African Tribe* (2 vols.). London, 1927.

Kalabo District Files

Kuntz, M. 'Les rites occultes et la sorcellerie sur le Haut-Zambèze.' *J. Soc. Africanistes,* II, 2, 1932.

Lane Poole, E. H. Unpublished manuscript on the tribes of Eastern Province, in the Rhodes-Livingstone Museum.

Mayer, P. *Witches.* Inaugural lecture delivered at Rhodes University, Grahamstown, 1954.

McCulloch, M. *The Southern Lunda and Related Peoples* (*Northern Rhodesia, Angola, Belgian Congo*). Ethnographic Survey of Africa, London, 1951.

Mankoya District Files

Melland, F. M. *In Witchbound Africa.* London, 1923.

Mongu District Files

Munday, J. T. *Witchcraft in England and in Central Africa,* in Munday, J. T., Vowles, E. M., and Broomfield, G. W., *Witchcraft.* London, 1951.

Munday, J. T., Vowles, E. M., and Broomfield, G.W. *Witchcraft.* London, 1951.

Northern Rhodesia Government. *Forest Department Check List* (*Vernacular/ Botanical Names*). Revised edition, Kitwe, 1956 (roneo).

    Records of proceedings in the Federal Supreme Court, Mongu. Livingstone, 1957 (roneo).

BIBLIOGRAPHY

    (a) Siyambo Twelve, Somili Muyawa and Musiluka Lifu Ngumune.
    (b) Lice Mwakoyi and Mwikisa Nawa.
    (c) William Kachana and Simenda Mwendanayo.
    Annual Reports for the year 1957. Lusaka, 1958.
        (a) African Affairs.
        (b) Department of Labour.

Parrinder, G. *Witchcraft.* London, 1958.

Reynolds, Barrie. *Barotse Witchcraft.* Livingstone, 1957 (roneo).
        'Kaliloze Night Guns.' *Nada*, Vol. 35, Salisbury, 1958.
        The Material Culture of the Peoples of the Gwembe Valley.
(In preparation.)

Richards, A. I. 'A modern movement of Witch-finders.' *Africa*, Vol. VIII, No. 4, London, 1935.

Rose, R. *Living Magic.* London, 1957.

Royal Anthropological Institute. *Notes and queries on Anthropology.* London, 1951.

Schapera, I. *The Khoisan Peoples of South Africa.* London, 1930.
        The Bantu-speaking Tribes of South Africa. London, 1937.

Seabrook, W. B. *The Magic Island.* London, 1929.
        Jungle Ways. London, 1931.

Senanga District Files

Sesheke District Files

Segy, L. 'Circle-Dot symbolic Sign on african Ivory Carvings.' *Zaire*, Vol. VII, No. 1, 1953.

Sigerist, H. E. *A History of Medicine.* Vol. I, *Primitive and Archaic Medicine.* New York, 1951.

Singleton-Fisher, W. 'Black Magic Feuds.' *African Studies*, Vol. 8, No. 1, Johannesburg, 1949.

Smith, E. W. and Dale, A. M. *The Ila-speaking Peoples of Northern Rhodesia* (2 vols.). London, 1920.

Symon, S. A. *Some Notes on the Preparation and Uses of Native Medicines in the Mankoya District.* 1950 (roneo). Also published as *African Medicine in the Mankoya District, Northern Rhodesia* in Rhodes Livingstone Communication No. 15. Lusaka, 1959.

Tracey, H. 'The Bones.' *Nada*, Vol. 12, Salisbury, 1934.

Turner, V. W. *The Lozi Peoples of North-Western Rhodesia.* Ethnographic Survey of Africa, London, 1952.
        Schism and Continuity in an African Society. Manchester, 1957.
        Ndembu Divination, its Symbolism and Techniques. Rhodes-Livingstone Paper No. 31, Manchester, 1961.

BIBLIOGRAPHY

Wagner, G. *The Bantu of North Kavirondo.* Vol. 1, London, 1949.

Wethey, I. H. *The Twelve Society*, in *Mongu District Files.* 1957.

White, C. M. N. 'The Supreme Being in the Beliefs of the Balovale Tribes.' *African Studies*, Vol. 7, No. 1, Johannesburg, 1948a.

'Witchcraft, Divination and Magic among the Balovale Tribes.' *Africa*, Vol. XVIII, No. 2, London, 1948b.

'Stratification and Modern Changes in an Ancestral Cult.' *Africa*, XIX, No. 4, London, 1949.

Elements in Luvale Beliefs and Rituals. Rhodes-Livingstone Paper No. 32, Manchester, 1961.

Wright, H. B. *Witness to Witchcraft.* London, 1958.

INDEX

INDEX

Frazer, Sir J. G., 51n
freemen, 9
Fwe, 7

G

Garbutt, H. W., 105
Gelfand, M., 15, 48n, 105n, 107, 107n, 108, 116n, 117, 119, 125, 126, 130, 130n, 131, 131n
genet, 65, 66, 125
Ghana, 16
Gilges, W., 62, 67
Gluckman, M., 6–10 passim, 18, 18n, 40, 40n, 65, 123, 125, 132n, 143
gods (see religious beliefs, Lesa, Nyambe, Nzambi)
gonorrhea, 66
Gouldsbury, C., and Sheane, H., 104
grave-robbing (see also necrophagy), 24–26 passim, 29, 29n, 43, 44–45
guilds, 23, 56–58

H

hallucinogenic drugs, 23n
hamba (see mahamba)
headaches, 49, 66, 67
headmen, 55, 149–150, 154, 158, 159
herbal doctors (see ng'aka)
hippopotamus, 38
Hoernlé, A. W., 104, 105n, 107n, 121n, 125, 131n
Hogg, G., 24
hospitals, 59, 77n
Hough, C. D., (see Fanshawe, D. B., and Hough, C. D.)
Humbe, 7
Hunt, N. A., 105n
Hunter, M., 163
hupa, 135
hyenas, 25, 39, 129, 130
doctor of (see ng'aka wa sitongwani)

I

Ila, 7, 104, 106, 124, 128, 163
ilomba, 33, 35–38, 39, 45
ilutwa (see Ximenia americana)
Imilangu, 7, 144, 145

indunas, 9, 59, 149, 158
inhalations, 64, 66, 69
initiation, 10, 26–27, 152
injections (see also needles), 59, 79
Investigations, 11–13
isanusi (see also 'smelling out'), 104

J

jackals, 38, 39
Jalla, A., 18n
jikenyenge (see lucky beans)
Junod, H. A., 80n, 105

K

Kabompo, R., 118
kahwehwi, (see also familiars, tuyebela), 29
kakundukundu (see whirlwind)
Kalabo, 1, 4, 6, 8, 9, 11–13, 39, 42, 42n, 74, 77, 85, 122, 125, 133, 134, 139, 141, 142, 143, 144, 145
kalankata, 34–35
Kalene Hill, 37
kaliloze, 11, 12, 20, 38, 39, 40, 53, 53n, 55, 74, 76, 77, 79–88, 95, 97, 121, 124, 140, 141, 142, 143, 145, 146, 163, 164
doctors (see kaliloze, kaliloze gunmen, ng'aka)
gunmen (see also kaliloze, ng'aka), 53–55, 56, 58, 76, 79, 139, 141, 142
Kalomo, 13
Kamanga, Rice (see Chana I)
kanameya (see nameya)
kanenga (see also familiars), 29, 31, 72, 118, 119
Kangala, 7
Kaonde, 7, 34, 35, 36, 39, 40n, 56, 115, 123, 124, 128
kapende, 126
kaponya (see also familiars), 29
kashiamusongo, 41, 42
kata, 86, 86n
Katima Mulilo, 1, 2, 4, 5
Kaunga, 9
kaututumbwa, 35
kayongo (see sisongo)
Kenya, 77
Kololo, 8, 106, 162
kuloze (see kaliloze)

Kunda, 19
Kuntz, M., 18, 18n, 25, 29n, 39, 43, 44n, 64, 95, 105, 114, 116, 118, 130
kuposa (see siposo)
kutas, 9, 141, 142
kuyata (see sikuyeti)
Kwandi, 7, 83, 86, 88, 89, 119, 144, 146
Kwangali, 7
Kwangwa, 7, 9, 72, 144, 145, 146
Kwanyama, 67n

L

labour (see migrant labour)
Labour Officer, Livingstone, 3n, 4n
labour rate, unskilled, 5
Labour Route, 2, 2n
Lamba, 111, 115, 117
Lane Poole, E. H., 18–20, 39
laryngitis, 35
Lawrance, J. G. (see District Commissioner, Senanga)
Laws of Northern Rhodesia, 48, 61, 139, 164, 164n, Appendix
lay specialist, 49–50, 140
Lealui, 9
leech (see ng'aka)
Lemon, J. O. (see District Commissioner, Kalabo)
Lesa, 10, 40n, 128
Lewanika (see also Paramount Chief), 1, 18n, 64, 123, 124, 129, 155
Concession, 1n
Libonda, 9
licences, 59–61
lightning, 40, 40n, 74, Chapter V passim, 145, 150
lihamba (see mahamba)
likishi (see also familiars), 29, 31, 72, 119
likwena (see crocodiles)
lilombamema (see ilomba)
Limulunga, 9
linkalankala, 34
Liondo village, 33
lion-men (see ng'aka wa litau)
lions, 39, 129
doctor of (see ng'aka wa litau)
litaula, 105n

177

INDEX

siposo (*see siposo*), 39–41
direct attack (*see direct attack*), 41–44
cannibalism and necrophagy (*see* cannibalism, necrophagy), 24–26, 44–47
court case records, Chapter VII *passim*
muloji (*see also muloi*), 14n
mulolo (*see ilomba*)
mulombe (*see ilomba*)
Mulonga, 7
mulyashinji (*see Capparis tomentosa*)
Mumbwa, 59
Munday, J. T., 22
mungongo (*see Ricinodendron rautenenii*; *also* divining nutshells)
munyonga (*see Ekebergia meyeri*)
mupitipiti (*see* lucky beans)
muroi (*see also muloi*), 15
musolu, 128
mutata (*see Securidaca longipedunculata*)
mutukule (*see muhole*)
mutulomuko, 42, 42n
muwewe (*see Sterculia sp.*), 80, 83
mwafi (*see also* divining, ordeal poison), 122, 123
mwanankishi (*see also* familiars) 29, 31, 119
Mwanawina III, Sir (*see also* Paramount Chief), 1
Mwandi, 9
mwavi (*see also* divining, ordeal poison), 122, 124
   wa wombwe (*see* divining, boiling water test), 124
mwazi (*see also* divining, ordeal poison), 122, 123
mwenda-lutaka (*see also muba*), 65
   -njangula (*see also muba*), 65
Mwenyi, 7, 37
mwevulu (*see also* spirits), 35
mwinda (*see Securidaca longipedunculata*)
Mwinilunga, 25, 36, 37, 79

N

Naliele, 9
Nalindele, 21–22
Nalolo, 9

nameya (*see also* familiars), 29, 33, 72, 119
Namwala, 59
namwemba, 66
Natal, 148n
Ndebele, 7, 8, 105, 106
ndeke (*see also mahamba*), 64, 133
Ndembu, 7, 18, 19, 36, 40n, 102n
ndumba (*see also* familiars), 16, 29, 29n, 43
ndume, 66
Ndundulu (*see* Imilangu)
necrophagers (*see muloi*, necrophagy)
necrophagy (*see also* cannibalism, *muloi*), Chapter II *et passim*:
   motives, 24–26
   initiation, 26–27
   methods and equipment, 44–46
   court case records, Chapter VII *passim*
needles, 12, 39, 40, 46n, 48, 59, 70, 74, 76–79, 97, 136, 136n, 140, 142–143, 145, 151–152, 155, 160, 163, 164
New Mbunda (*see* Mbunda)
ng'aka, Chapter III *et passim*:
   definition, 48–50
   female doctors, 52
   motives, selection, training, 52–55
   witchdoctors and sorcerers, 55–56
   witchdoctors and diviners, 56, 95
   guilds, 56–58
   doctors and society, 58–61, 94
   itinerants, 58–59, 148
   borrowings from European doctors, 59
   licences, 59–61
   witchfinders and diviners, 95
   causes of misfortune, 61–69:
      ancestral spirits, 62–64
      mahamba, 63–64
      bush spirits, 64–66
      muba, 65–66
      physical causes, 66–69
      baloi, 69

weapons and methods, 69–90:
   protective magic, 69–70
   punitive protection, 70–72
   familiars, 72
   siposo, 72–74
   needles, 76–79
   kaliloze, 79–88
   sikuyeti, 88–90
dress and equipment, 90–94
court case records, Chapter VII *passim*
wa likwena (*see also sitondo*), 129–130
wa litau (*see also sitondo*), 39, 129–130
wa pula (*see also sitondo*), 129, 130
wa sitongwani (*see also sitondo*), 129–130
ya buloi (*see also ng'aka*), 49, 129
nganga (*see also muloi*), 14n, 48n
   (*see also ng'aka*), 14n, 48n, 110, 117, 119, 126, 130
Nganguela, 116n
ngoba bracelets, 41, 74
ngombo (*see* divining *ngombo*)
Ngoni, 7
Nguni, 104
nguvu (*see* hippopotamus)
nightjars, 39
night guns (*see kaliloze*)
nkala (*see* crabs)
Nkoya, 7, 8, 33, 36, 83, 118, 144, 145, 145n, 146
Nkoya, 7, 9
Northern Province, 122
Northern Rhodesia Government (*see also* administration), 1, 4, 4n, 6, 12n, 20, 81, 82
North-Western Province, 1, 77, 123
Nsenga, 18ff, 39
Nyambe, 10, 129
Nyanswa, 7
Nyasaland, 77
Nyemba, 116n
Nyengo, 7
nyunywani (*see* birds)
Nzambi, 128
nzila, 101
nzovu (*see* elephant)

INDEX